New Jersey
Off the Beaten Path™

Praise for earlier editions:

"This unique book concentrates . . . on N.J.'s wonderful weirdness."
> —*New York Daily News*

"Has interesting anecdotes along with its destinations."
> —*Hackensack* (N.J.) *Sunday Record*

D0651001

OFF THE BEATEN PATH™ SERIES

New Jersey

FOURTH EDITION

Off the Beaten Path™

William G. and
Kay Scheller

The Globe Pequot Press

Old Saybrook, Connecticut

Copyright © 1988, 1991, 1995, 1998 by William G. Scheller

All rights reserved. No part of this book may be reproduced or transmitted in any form by any means, electronic or mechanical, including photocopying and recording, or by any information storage and retrieval system, except as may be expressly permitted by the 1976 Copyright Act or by the publisher. Requests for permission should be made in writing to The Globe Pequot Press, P.O. Box 833, Old Saybrook, Connecticut 06475.

Maps created by Equator Graphics © The Globe Pequot Press
Illustrations by Carole Drong
Cover and text design by Laura Augustine
Cover photo: Images© PhotoDisc, Inc.

Off the Beaten Path is a trademark of The Globe Pequot Press.

Library of Congress Cataloging-in-Publication Data

Scheller, William.
     New Jersey : off the beaten path / William G. and Kay Scheller.
     p. cm. —(Off the beaten path series)
  Includes index.
  ISBN 0-7627-0194-3
  1. New Jersey—Guidebooks. I. Scheller, Kay. II. Title.
  III. Series.
  F132.3.S34   1998
  917.4904'43—dc21

                                  97-52956
                                      CIP

Manufactured in the United States of America
Fourth Edition/Second Printing

To Alice and William G. Scheller, two New Jerseyans who helped immensely in researching and revising this book

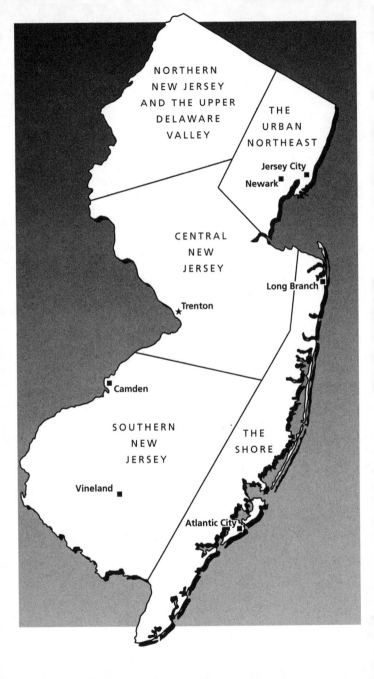

Contents

Help Us Keep This Guide Up to Date

Every effort has been made by the author and editors to make this guide as accurate and useful as possible. However, many things can change after a guide is published—establishments close, phone numbers change, facilities come under new management, etc.

We would love to hear from you concerning your experiences with this guide and how you feel it could be made better and be kept up to date. While we may not be able to respond to all comments and suggestions, we'll take them to heart and we'll also make certain to share them with the author. Please send your comments and suggestions to the following address:

The Globe Pequot Press
Reader Response/Editorial Department
P.O. Box 833
Old Saybrook, CT 06475

Or you may e-mail us at:

editorial@globe-pequot.com

Thanks for your input, and happy travels!

Introduction

Nineteen ninety-eight marks the tenth anniversary of the first publication of *New Jersey: Off the Beaten Path™*. It was hard to believe that there had been this much water under the bridge (think of the Hackensack River flowing beneath the Pulaski Skyway), until we went looking for the floppy disk with the text of the first edition and discovered there was no such thing: It had been written on a typewriter.

This ten-year benchmark for *NJ: OBP* is not only an occasion for reflection on the book and how it's changed, but for thinking about how the Garden State itself has been transformed during the last decade of the twentieth century. Although the population boom in this most densely populated of states has somewhat abated—there are a million more New Jerseyans than there were thirty years ago, but that rate of increase is way down from the million-per-decade midcentury surge—there have nonetheless been significant shifts in where people live in the Garden State, where they come from, and in their lifestyles. Parts of Sussex County that were pasture and cropland ten years ago now sprout housing developments; and old immigrant cities like Paterson seem to have added a new ethnic dimension each time we go back for another look. (At Eastertime 1997, we wandered around what we thought was a long-disused part of the Silk City's downtown, and found it abustle with businesses ranging from African groceries to a Caribbean seafood market selling fresh parrotfish.) In parts of Hoboken and Jersey City where all there used to be were dreary railroad flats (a kind of tenement apartment in which one room led straight into another), there are now snazzy condos within walking distance of wine shops that sell a lot more than cheap muscatel.

But much of New Jersey has stayed the same. We took a special delight, during the summer of '97, in introducing our son David to what remains one of the most beautiful beaches in the world: the 120-mile stretch of white sand that extends from Sandy Hook to Cape May, where the ocean is bracing but (at least by July) never forbiddingly frigid; where good Italian restaurants are as thick as they are in Naples; and where you can turn your back on the machines that ate your quarters in Atlantic City and enjoy gorgeous expanses of federally protected salt marsh. The Pine Barrens, the heart of which has also been protected from development, are still splendidly desolate almost to the point of eeriness, and the exurban lanes of southwest Jersey, around Greenwich, are in much the same league as the byways of up-country New England, even if the terrain is a bit flatter. If you want more rugged country, there are always the Kittatinny Mountains that stand sentinel above the Delaware Water Gap, away up north near the New York and Pennsylvania borders.

For such a small state, New Jersey has a tremendously varied topography. The black basalt cliffs called the Palisades tower formidably above the Hudson River at the state's northeastern gateway and slope westward toward the great marshy basin of the Hackensack Meadows. More than 270 species of birds have been observed in the Meadows, hundreds of acres of which have been preserved despite the encroachment of condos, office parks, and Giants Stadium. The Great Swamp, near

Chatham and Summit in the north-central part of the state, is the site of an even more impressive preservation effort. Here more than 6,000 acres of primeval freshwater wetlands were set aside under federal protection after citizens rallied, more than thirty years ago, to keep out a projected jetport.

Nor has New Jersey any apologies to make when it comes to historical associations. This was an old and well-settled place by the time of the American Revolution; during the century and a half that went before, Dutch and English settlers in the north and Swedes in the south had been hewing farms and homes out of the land of the Lenni-Lenape Indians. Men smelted iron in the Pine Barrens and the Ramapo Mountains in the middle of the eighteenth century, and the Revolution was barely over when Alexander Hamilton stood at the Great Falls of the Passaic and decided that here would be built America's first planned industrial city.

All too often we tend to limit our geographical notions of the War for Independence to the early battlefields of Massachusetts and the political arenas of Philadelphia, but more of that eight-year struggle took place in New Jersey than anywhere else, and the state well earned its title "Cockpit of the Revolution." Here the Continental army waited out winters as devastating to morale as the one at Valley Forge; here George Washington accomplished what has been called the greatest strategic retreat in military history; and here, at Christmastime in 1777, the American commander-in-chief won the Battle of Trenton after his legendary crossing of the Delaware.

New Jersey's role in the Industrial Revolution was no less impressive. Basic, resource-extraction enterprises, such as the mines at Ringwood and Batsto, soon began to be eclipsed by manufacturing, with Paterson rising to become the nation's preeminent weaver of silk and its second-most important builder of locomotives (after Philadelphia). Railroads have figured prominently in New Jersey ever since John Stevens demonstrated America's first working steam locomotive on his Hoboken estate in 1824. The state became vital to rail enterprises such as the Pennsylvania and Erie railroads and the Delaware, Lackawanna, and Western, which operated electric passenger trains perfected by the Wizard of Menlo Park (New Jersey), Thomas Edison. Today the petroleum, petrochemical, and pharmaceutical industries are among the state's largest employers.

The purpose of this book is to distill New Jersey's diversity—geographic, ethnic, historical, and industrial—into the description of selected sites in the five major areas of the state. These places haven't been chosen because they're the preeminent New Jersey attractions; the premise of the Off the Beaten Path series is the discovery of places many guidebooks overlook. You'll find some familiar spots, but our hope is that most of the territory covered in these pages will be as new as the perceptions it may inspire. If, while following this guide, you drive along the turnpike, eat in a diner on Route 9, and pop a Bruce Springsteen tape into the cassette deck, that's all right. Just remember, there's a lot more to New Jersey than those stereotypical experiences suggest.

Several of the additions to this edition of *NJ: OBP* reflect changes designed to make the entire Off the Beaten Path series more comprehensive as practical travel guides, even though our emphasis continues to be upon the unusual. These include a brief summary of the state's top attractions and of smaller sites not described in the text; region-by-region listings of hotels, inns, restaurants, visitor information centers, and events; and a slate of New Jersey facts, statistics, and logistical information.

We hope you enjoy exploring New Jersey as much as we have—and that the twentieth anniversary edition of *NJ: OBP* finds the Pine Barrens just as desolate, the surf at Ship Bottom every bit as invigorating, and the Paterson markets stuffed with the ingredients of cuisines we haven't even heard of yet, much less sampled.

Although thorough efforts have been made to verify hours of operation and admission charges and rates, these items often change at the whim of proprietors or as a result of governmental budgets. Therefore, call ahead for current information before traveling.

New Jersey Information

Travel information

New Jersey Division of Travel & Tourism
20 West State Street, Trenton 08625;
(800) JERSEY7 or (609) 292–2470
Web site: http://www.state.nj.us/travel

B&B Innkeepers Association of New Jersey, Inc.
P.O. Box 108T
Spring Lake 07762;
(908) 449–3535
(a free directory is available)

New Jersey Room Reservations: for resorts, hotels,
motels, B&Bs, and country inns throughout the
state;
(800) 365–6965

New Jersey Campground Association
29 Cooks Beach Road
Cape May Court House 08210;
(800) 2–CAMP–NJ for free guide

Temperatures average

32.1 degrees Fahrenheit December–February
51.6 degrees Fahrenheit March–May
74.4 degrees Fahrenheit June–August
57.1 degrees Fahrenheit September–November

Transportation

Major Airports:
Atlantic City International Airport,
(609) 645–7895
Newark International Airport, (973) 961–6000

XV

Trains:
    AMTRAK, (800) USA-RAIL
    New Jersey Transit Passenger Rail System:
        Northern New Jersey, (800) 772–2222;
            out-of-state, (800) 762–5100
        Southern New Jersey, (800) 582–5946;
            out-of-state, (215) 569–3752

Major newspapers

Jersey Journal (Jersey City)
Newark Star Ledger (Newark)
Herald News (Passaic County)
Bergen Record (Hackensack)
Philadelphia Inquirer (Philadelphia,
    Pennsylvania—read widely in Southern
    New Jersey)

Population

7,945,298 (1995 census); New Jersey ranks ninth in
    population in the United States

Some Selected World Wide Web Addresses in New Jersey

General information:
http://www.state.nj.us

Free travel publications:
http://www.state.nj.us/travel/free pub.html

State-wide events and New Jersey Transit information:
http://www.state.nj.us/travel/calendar/html

Weather:
http://www.climate.rutgers.edu/stateclim/for.html

Bed & Breakfast Innkeepers Association:
http://www.bbianj.com/

New Jersey Audubon Society:
http://www.njcom/audubon/

New Jersey Campground Owners Association:
http://www.beachcomber.com/nj/campnj.html

New Jersey Road Map:
http://www.online96.com/towns/lbi/njmap.html

The Urban Northeast

New Jersey's heavily urbanized northeastern corner often serves the popular imagination as a metaphor for the entire state. It might just as well represent all the United States—not because the entire country is as densely populated as New Jersey, but because, at its best, it is as richly textured and heterogeneous as New Jersey's contribution to the New York metropolitan area. One of the most striking aspects of this compact region is its racial and ethnic diversity; remember that Ellis Island is only a few hundred yards from Jersey City. People come here, people stay, people pass through on their way to somewhere else (Union City, once a Swiss preserve, is now largely a Cuban community). Within this chapter we'll visit the home of an Italian labor organizer, farmhouses that belonged to the earliest Dutch settlers, and a rich display of African art and artifacts.

Dense population, with the complicated patchwork of cities, suburbs, and industrial districts that it engenders, seldom gets good press, and there's no denying that it has spawned its share of problems. But an often-overlooked virtue of the Jersey metropolis is its variety, the quickness with which one environment gives way to another. When so many towns and cities are this close together, even locals usually have to admit that there is plenty they haven't seen (or maybe

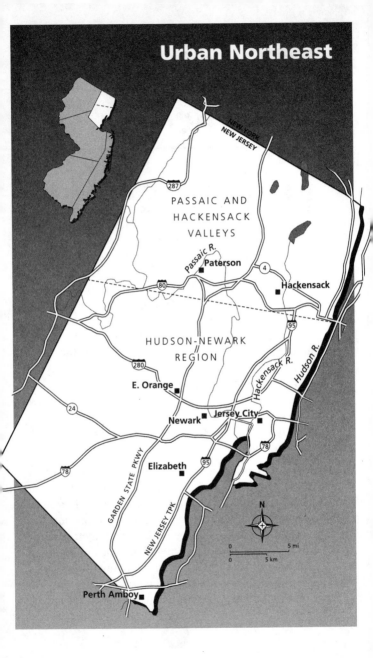

Urban Northeast

PASSAIC AND HACKENSACK VALLEYS

NEW YORK
NEW JERSEY

Passaic R.

Paterson

Hackensack

HUDSON-NEWARK REGION

Hackensack R.

Hudson R.

E. Orange

Newark

Jersey City

Elizabeth

GARDEN STATE PKWY

NEW JERSEY TPK

Perth Amboy

N

0   5 mi
0   5 km

THE URBAN NORTHEAST'S TOP PICKS

Palisades

Waterford Gardens

Hiram Blauvelt Art Museum

Steuben House

USS Ling

The African Art Museum of the S.M.A. Fathers

Great Falls/S.U.M. National Historic Landmark District

Lambert Castle

American Labor Museum

Van Riper–Hopper Museum

William Paterson College

Dey Mansion

The Montclair Art Museum

Presby Iris Gardens

Aviation Hall of Fame and Museum of New Jersey

Turkish Kitchen

Park Performing Arts Center

Clam Broth House

Afro-American Historical Society Museum

Statue of Liberty

South Mountain Reservation

Turtle Back Zoo

Watchung Reservation

First Presbyterian Church

Bible Gardens of Israel

even heard of) right within their county limits. Distances don't shrink under these circumstances; they expand: People in eastern Wyoming probably know more about western Wyoming than the folks in Hoboken know about Hackensack.

Note: The orientation in this chapter is roughly north to south.

Passaic and Hackensack Valleys

The **Palisades** are the dark, beetling cliffs that begin near the border of Hudson and Bergen Counties and continue northward into New York State. The Palisades are more than just the foreground for the Jersey sunsets that sell terraced Manhattan apartments; they are a window into deep geological time and the focus of one of the region's earliest and most successful preservation movements. They're also a great place to take a hike.

By the mid-nineteenth century extensive quarrying operations were set up, and before long the southerly reaches of the cliffs were all but obliterated. Fortunately, early preservation activists persuaded the states of New York and New Jersey to purchase the Palisades, along with the land at their base and summit. Quarrying stopped in 1900, and by 1909 **Palisades Interstate Park** had been dedicated.

The best way to enjoy the Palisades today is to hike along either the Long Path, which runs along the crest of

AUTHORS' FAVORITE ATTRACTIONS IN THE URBAN NORTHEAST

African Art Museum of the S.M.A. Fathers
American Labor Museum
Hiram Blauvelt Art Museum
Steuben House
William Paterson College

TOP EVENTS IN THE URBAN NORTHEAST

Note: Schedules may vary; call ahead.
St. Ann's Italian Festival, Hoboken; July; (201) 963–3780 or 659–1116
Hambletonian Day, Meadowlands Racetrack, East Rutherford; August; (201) 935–8500
Newark Jazz Festival, Newark; November; (973) 643–3605

the cliffs and offers lovely views of the Hudson and the New York shore, or the Shore Path, which follows the riverbank at the base of the towering rocks. To begin the latter route, which is marked with white blazes and extends 10 miles northward into New York State, park at the Englewood Boat Basin, just north of the New Jersey approach to the George Washington Bridge. A good access point for the Long Path is 5 miles north (via Route 9W) at the turnoff for the Alpine Boat Basin. At Alpine, both trails are connected by a steep switchback path. Whatever you do, stick to marked paths such as this one when ascending or descending in the Palisades. Much of the rock is loose and makes for extremely dangerous climbing.

Waterford Gardens in Saddle River is likely to be different from any garden center you've ever seen. Its exclusive focus is water plants—day- and night-blooming tropical water lilies, lotus, floating plants, and aquatic border plants—as well as ornamental fish.

The company's displays of its living wares are beautifully arranged along the banks of the Saddle River, in an array of ponds and pools that are more suggestive of a pristine bayou than the vicinity of exit 163 on the Garden State Parkway. Best of all, you don't have to be shopping for water lilies to visit the gardens. They're open to casual visitors—although we suspect that many of those visitors won't be so casual once they start thinking about the possibilities of water gardening and that lily ponds will start appearing in more and more suburban backyards.

Waterford Gardens, 74 East Allendale Road, Saddle River 07458, (201) 327–0721, is open Monday through Saturday 8:00 A.M.–5:00 P.M. and Sunday 9:00 A.M.–4:00 P.M., mid-April through August 31; the rest of the year, Monday through Saturday 9:00 A.M.–5:00 P.M. Admission is free.

If a walk among the ancient rocks of the Palisades inspires an appreciation of New Jersey's prehistory, you can learn more at the *Bergen Museum of Art and Science* in Paramus. The museum houses specimens of the various rock formations that characterize the area, as well as fossils indigenous to North Jersey and even parts of the skeleton of an early local inhabitant, the Hackensack Mastodon. A separate museum collection comprises artifacts that document the lives of the Lenni-

The Making of the Palisades

*T**he grand, dark cliffs called the Palisades, which dominate the New Jersey side of the Hudson River from the George Washington Bridge to the New York State border and beyond, had their origin 190 million years ago, when molten rock forced its way upward into fissures in layers of sandstone and shale. The molten material cooled beneath the surface, hardening into a rock called diabase, before being exposed by erosion. The columnar, prismlike structure of the cliffs is a result of the contraction and vertical splintering that took place as the rock solidified. That structure also gave the formation its name—to early settlers, the cliffs resembled a palisade, a military enclosure made of sharpened stakes driven into the ground.*

Lenape Indians, a Delaware-related tribe that was already established in Bergen County 12,000 years ago.

In other parts of this intimate museum, the emphasis is on art, with constantly changing exhibits of what it calls "Up Art"—that is, art that lifts the spirits. A series of free Sunday afternoon concerts, a Nature Room that houses live specimens of small animals native to the Bergen area, a broad range of children's programs, theatrical presentations, and a variety of lectures and programs for adults make the Bergen Museum the most active and well-attended museum in the county.

The Bergen Museum of Art and Science, 327 East Ridgewood Avenue, Paramus 07652, (201) 265–1248, is open Tuesday through Saturday 9:30 A.M.–4:30 P.M. and Sunday 1:00–5:00 P.M. Suggested donation is $2.50 for adults, $1.00 for children, students, and senior citizens.

Step into a world where elephants roam the African veldt, Canada geese glide tranquilly across fog-shrouded ponds, and a snow leopard looks down from his lofty perch high in the Himalayas. In 1957 conservationist Hiram Blauvelt donated his private wildlife art and big-game collection to focus awareness on issues facing the natural world, and to showcase the artists who are inspired by it. Today, the *Hiram Blauvelt Art Museum,* in Mr. Blauvelt's 1893 turreted, shingle-style carriage house, exhibits a large collection of Audubon folios, works by artists such as Carl Rungius and Charles Livingston Bull, and magnificent dioramas. The big-game collection includes a large display of North American mammals.

The Hiram Blauvelt Art Museum, 705 Kinderkamack Road, Oradell 07649, (201) 261–0012, is open Wednesday, Thursday, and Friday 10:00 A.M. to 4:00 P.M., and Saturday and Sunday from 2:00 to 5:00 P.M. Closed holidays. Admission is free.

Although the *Steuben House* was named for the Prussian-born hero of the American Revolution, Major General Baron Friedrich von Steuben, the house dates to 1713, well before the general's birth.

The oldest part of the house was built by Johannes Ackerman of Hackensack. In 1752 a new owner, Jan Zabriskie, expanded the building to its present size and gave it its graceful gambrel roof. In 1939 the structure was restored and opened as a museum.

The Steuben House is an appropriate showplace for the collections of the Bergen County Historical Society, which include eighteenth-century furnishings and a trove of antique toys distinguished by what is said to be the oldest doll in the United States—"Betsy Coxe"—made of wax about the year 1700.

Directly in front of the Steuben House is an 1888 iron bridge (closed to traffic) occupying the site of the original "New Bridge"of 1774 that figured so prominently in the retreat of American troops late in 1776.

The Steuben House, 1209 Main Street, River Edge 07661, (201) 487-1739, is open Wednesday through Saturday 10:00 A.M. to noon and 1:00 to 5:00 P.M.; Sunday 2:00 to 5:00 P.M. Admission is free.

Just a few miles downriver from Steuben House is a relic of another war—the submarine **USS *Ling,*** riding peacefully at anchor in the Hackensack River. The *Ling* was brought here for restoration in 1973 by the Submarine Memorial Association after being decommissioned by the U.S. Navy in 1971.

The 312-foot *Ling* was commissioned in June 1945, during the closing days of World War II. She made one Atlantic patrol before the war's end and was kept in reserve until her recommissioning in 1960 as a naval training vessel. Her home port during this era was the Brooklyn Navy Yard, from which she made her last voyage, through New York Harbor and Newark Bay into the tidal mouth of the Hackensack, after the Navy agreed to donate the vessel to the Memorial Association rather than consign her to scrap.

The *Ling* stands as a monument to the diesel era of American submarine operations and to the men who served as submariners. She has 2,040 tons displacement,

The USS *Ling* is a World War II diesel submarine decommissioned by the U.S. Navy in 1971.

6,400 horsepower, with accommodations for twenty-four torpedoes and a crew of ninety-five officers and men. Visitors can board the *Ling* and see the engine and control rooms, the torpedo rooms, and the close quarters of the crew.

The USS *Ling* and adjacent Naval Museum, Borg Park, Court and River Streets, Hackensack 07601, (201) 342–3268, opens at 10:00 A.M. Wednesday through Sunday year-round (last tour at 4:00 P.M.). Admission is $4.00 for adults, $2.50 for children under twelve.

Traditionally, many Christian missionaries to Africa regarded the peoples and cultures among whom they worked as inferior to those of the West. Their artifacts were often judged ugly, and objects having any connection with so-called pagan religious practices were often collected and burned.

At **The African Art Museum of the S.M.A. Fathers,** the Society of African Missions in the United States instead offers a display of art and artifacts that emphasize the beauty and richness of African cultural expression.

Wandering about the museum, we learn that masks of the Wee people in Liberia, which may at first glimpse seem strange or grotesque, were in fact used as a social control. Each mask represented a specific spirit who wanted to be involved in human affairs. The masks were teachers of the values of tradition and law and the need to preserve those values. Helmet masks of the Baule in the Ivory Coast, which represent horned animals, are used in dances to protect the village, discipline women, and at funeral ceremonies.

The African Art Museum of the Society of African Missions (S.M.A.), 25 Bliss Avenue, Tenafly 07670, (201) 567–0450 (weekdays only), is open daily from 10:00 A.M. to 5:00 P.M. Donations are welcome.

Flat Rock Brook Nature Center is an oasis in the urban north, a 150-acre nature preserve with volcanic bedrock formations, cliffs, ponds, and meadows that's home to diverse plant and animal life. There are 3.2 miles of hiking trails (maps are available), and small kids will love the 800-foot Quarry Boardwalk in front of the center. At 443 Van Nostrand Avenue, Englewood, (201) 567–1265. The office is open daily 9:00 A.M. to 5:00 P.M. Picnic area and trails are open from sunrise to sunset. Admission is free.

If the Carp Are Jumping, It's Springtime on the Passaic

*A*ll too often, North Jersey's Passaic River is portrayed as an example of an urban waterway lost to pollution and streamside blight. But the Passaic does have its pristine stretches. It rises near the Great Swamp and passes through part of that wilderness preserve. Farther downstream the Passaic meanders through an area on the borders of Essex and Passaic counties called Great Piece Meadow—not a meadow so much as an impenetrable swamp, all the more remarkable for being within a few miles of Route 46 and the giant Willowbrook Mall.

About the only way to get into the heart of Great Piece is by canoe. We've done it in early April, and seen one of the true primeval spectacles of northern New Jersey: carp, usually thought of as sedate bottom feeders, jumping like trout during their spring spawning season.

The Passaic Falls, located in the heart of the city that they created—Paterson—are the focus of the *Great Falls/S.U.M. National Historic Landmark District.* ("S.U.M." stands for Society for the Establishment of Useful Manufactures, the industrial development organization founded along with Paterson in 1791.)

Here the waters of the Passaic River, which has its source nearly 50 miles upstream in the Great Swamp, crash over a 280-foot-wide chasm to continue toward tidewater at Newark Bay. During the Revolution on July 10, 1778, George Washington and Alexander Hamilton came to stand on the rock ledge opposite the falls and marvel at their fury. To Hamilton, however, the falls were more than a scenic wonder. Once independence was won, he was quick to propose that the waters of the Passaic should be harnessed as a source of power for the nation's first planned industrial city. In 1791 the settlement above and below the cataract was incorporated and named for William Paterson, New Jersey governor and signer of the Declaration of Independence.

Paterson's founders selected French engineer Pierre L'Enfant to design Paterson's industrial infrastructure. L'Enfant came up with an ingenious system of raceways, but the plan was never completed to his specifications due to its considerable expense. Eventually Connecticut industrialist Peter Colt finished the job. It was well into the 1820s before Paterson's first significant industry— cotton—gained a foothold, but before long the millraces were supplying waterpower to a host of burgeoning enterprises. The locomotive industry would prosper here throughout the remainder of the nineteenth century, and the silk industry even longer. By 1900 the "Silk City" would be the fifteenth largest in the United States.

The Great Falls Historic District is primarily concerned with the legacy of Paterson's industrial heyday. Sites within the district include the falls themselves and several of the more important mills that once dominated the area: The **Rogers Locomotive Erecting Shop** (now housing the Paterson Museum, described below); the wheelhouse of the **Ivanhoe Paper Mill**; the **home of John Ryle,** who first introduced silk manufacturing to Paterson; the **Benjamin Thompsen House** (circa 1835); the **Phoenix Mill Complex**; the two remaining stories of the 1836 mill in which Samuel Colt built his first regular production revolvers; and the impressive Beaux Arts **City Hall.**

Guided group tours start at the **Great Falls Visitor Center,** 65 McBride Avenue, Paterson 07501, (973) 279-9587. The center is open Monday through Friday 9:00 A.M.–4:00 P.M. and on Sunday, from April through September, noon–4:00 P.M.

The **Paterson Museum**'s collections of photographs and artifacts document the textile and locomotive-building industries, as well as Paterson's short-lived involvement in Samuel Colt's firearms enterprise. Perhaps the most famous of the museum's holdings, however, are the two earliest experimental submarines, built in 1878 and 1881 by John P. Holland, father of the modern submarine. The museum's interests also range to the natural and social history of the North Jersey area.

Finally, two most fitting exhibits stand in the courtyard outside the Paterson Museum building—Alco-Cooke locomotives, built just across Market Street from the Rogers plant. Number 299 was built in 1906 to help in the construction of the Panama Canal.

The Paterson Museum, 2 Market Street, Paterson 07501, (973) 881- 3839, is open Tuesday through Friday 10:00 A.M.–4:00 P.M.; Saturdays and Sundays 12:30–4:30 P.M. There is a suggested donation of $2.00 for adults.

In its industrial glory days at the turn of the century, Paterson supported a comfortable capitalist class. None

A Bad Year for Paterson

*O*n February 8, 1902, fire broke out in the streetcar barns near Paterson's Market Street. By the time the blaze was extinguished, the Silk City had lost nearly five hundred buildings, including the heart of the business district. The city's Beaux Arts City Hall, then only eight years old, was heavily damaged—it survives today, but with extensive postfire renovation.

Patersonians were barely beginning to tally the damages when, on March 2, the Passaic River roiled over its banks and carried away many of the mills, homes, and bridges that had not been lost in the fire.

of the silk barons lived so lavishly as Catholina Lambert, a man whose home, appropriately enough, has come to be called **Lambert Castle.** Today the home of the Passaic County Historical Society, this great sandstone pile still stands in lordly isolation on the brow of Garret Mountain, looking down over the mills and the city that made its builder rich.

Lambert built his Garret Mountain castle, which he called Belle Vista, in 1892; four years later he built the 70-foot tower (closed to visitors now) that still stands behind the house. Belle Vista became more than a home for Lambert and his family; it was also a magnificent history museum. Lambert died at the castle in 1923, at nearly ninety years of age. His house and grounds were acquired by the Passaic County Park Commission in 1928, and the building was opened as a museum six years later.

Lambert Castle, in Paterson, was built at the turn of the century by silk-baron Catholina Lambert.

In 1997 the castle and grounds underwent a $5.5 million restoration. The first floor of the castle is now interpreted as a historic house, with period rooms and an exhibit on Catholina Lambert. The art gallery on the second floor traces the development of Passaic County. There's also a newly restored three-story atrium/art court. A research library in the basement is open by appointment. The castle also serves as an excellent starting point for an exploration of the 575-acre *Garret Mountain Reservation,* jewel of the county's park system.

The Lambert Castle Museum is on Valley Road, Paterson 07503, (973) 881–2761. Call for hours and fees.

The other side of Paterson's industrial past is told in a far less imposing structure located in the nearby town of Haledon. This is the 1908 Victorian home of Italian

16

immigrants and mill workers Pietro and Mario Botto. Designated a national landmark, the Botto house is home to the ***American Labor Museum.***

The Bottos were silk workers carrying on a trade learned in the "Old Country," Italy. It was a tough life. Workers suffered with low wages, long hours, poor lighting, and harsh production demands. In 1913, when one of Paterson's companies tried to introduce the four-loom weaving system, workers realized that at least half of them would be put out of work. Spontaneously, they walked off their jobs and onto picket lines. One by one the mills were closed by the strikes and 25,000 people were out of work.

During the 1913 Paterson silk strike, Pietro Botto opened his doors to leaders of the Industrial Workers of the World (the IWW or "Wobblies"), such as William "Big Bill" Haywood and Elizabeth Gurley Flynn. While the strike lasted, thousands of Paterson millworkers would stand outside the house while Haywood and the others stirred them with oratory from its balcony.

The American Labor Museum's collections of photographs, union memorabilia, tools, and household artifacts document not only the silk strike itself, but the way of life of a generation of working-class immigrants.

The American Labor Museum/Botto House National Landmark, 83 Norwood Street, Haledon 07508, (973) 595–7953, is open Wednesday through Saturday 1:00 to 4:00 P.M. Admission is $1.50 for adults; free for children under twelve. Come at least forty-five minutes before closing time.

The **Van Riper–Hopper Museum** in Wayne is a fine example of New Jersey Dutch Colonial architecture. The one-and-one-half-story building, built in 1786 by Uriah Van Riper, has five lower rooms and four upstairs bedrooms in the main section of the house. The three rooms in the frame section are the former slave quarters. Typical of the New Jersey Dutch style, the house faces south, and the majority of windows are in the front to receive full benefit of sunlight. As was the custom with Dutch houses of the time, all additions were made to the side of the house rather than the rear.

Home-Fries Memories

*G*rowing up in Paterson in the 1950s, I lived just a few blocks from a factory that turned out one of New Jersey's most famous products—diners. Standing on East Twenty-seventh Street and watching a gleaming, freshly minted stainless-steel eatery roll out of the Silk City Diner Company's plant was every bit as exciting as watching a new battleship slide down the ways. After all, I had a proprietary interest in Silk City diners: My grandfather, John Marchitti, owned one. For two decades his Hiway Diner, on Route 4 in nearby Fairlawn, was a beacon to truckers, salesmen, families, and travelers of all sorts. I learned how to make home fries at the Hiway and how to craft the perfect Taylor ham and egg sandwich. A world that could use more of John Marchitti's counterside jokes hasn't heard them for nearly thirty years now, and I'm told that the Hiway Diner is someplace out in Pennsylvania. If any readers know just where, let me know and I'll be off quicker than it takes to fire up a griddle.

—Bill Scheller

There are six fireplaces throughout the house. During the year the fire in the huge basement fireplace, which contains a Dutch oven, was never allowed to die out for fear it would bring bad luck. Only on New Year's Day was the fireplace cleaned out, and then a new fire was promptly built.

The walls in the Van Riper–Hopper House are 20 inches thick and made of local fieldstone. The floors are wide pine planks. Open ceilings are supported by heavy hand-hewn beams. A mortar of clay, straw, and hair holds the stone walls in place, and the plaster of the inside walls is an inch thick.

The homestead was saved from destruction in 1964 after the Passaic Valley Water Commission planned the *Pointview Reservoir,* which now provides a waterfowl sanctuary and attracts devoted bird-watchers (who still reminisce about the rare sighting of a Hudsonian godwit). Flower and herb gardens are maintained by Wayne garden clubs.

Colonial hearth-cooking demonstrations are held periodically at the *Mead–Van Duyne Museum,* a Colonial stone house, which was moved 7 miles to the grounds of the Van Riper–Hopper House in 1974 to make room for highway expansion.

The Van Riper–Hopper House, 533 Berdan Avenue, Wayne 07470, (973) 694–7192, is open Friday through Tuesday, 1:00–4:00 P.M.; closed Wednesday and Thursday. A small donation is expected.

You may love some of the fourteen sculptures on the campus of *William Paterson College* . . . you may love them all . . . or you may hate them all. But as long as you

Who Needs Niagra?

*P*aterson's Great Falls of the Passaic River—one of the largest waterfalls east of the Mississippi—was chosen one of the ten most beautiful places in New Jersey in the May 1997 issue of New Jersey Monthly.

have some feeling about them, they've served their purpose. They've all been chosen as part of the school's Sculpture on Campus program, initiated to create an environment in which sculpture—whose development has generally been perceived as provocative and controversial—can be discovered, discussed, and, if necessary, challenged. Among them: Albert E. Henselmann's *Untitled*, Lyman Kipp's *Yoakum Jack*, Michel Gerard's *Mary Ellen Kramer Memorial Sculpture*, and Tova Beck-Friedman's *Magna Dea*.

The college's **Ben Shahn Galleries** host twelve contemporary exhibits a year, in a wide variety of mediums including painting, photography, ceramics, and computer-generated works. The gallery hosts an Art at Lunch slide/lecture series seven Thursdays each semester. Call for a schedule.

The William Paterson College of New Jersey is on Pompton Road in Wayne 07470, (973) 720-2371. The Ben Shahn Galleries (973-720-2654) are open September to the end of May, Monday through Friday, 10:00 A.M.–5:00 P.M.

There is a house in Wayne where George Washington not only slept but spent part of 1780 planning strategy as the

Revolution drew toward its decisive final year. This is the **Dey Mansion,** a graceful brick Georgian home, built about 1740 for Bergen County militia commander Colonel Theunis Dey. A visit here is as instructive of how a comfortable country family lived in America in the latter half of the eighteenth century as it is of the circumstances in which the commander-in-chief conducted his councils of war and lived out his days far from his own Virginia home. Period furnishings, weapons, prints, and documents all help to tell the tale.

The Dey (pronounced "die") Mansion, 199 Totowa Road, Wayne 07470, (973) 696–1776, is open Wednesday through Friday 1:00–4:00 P.M. and Saturday and Sunday 10:00 A.M.–noon and 1:00–4:00 P.M. Admission is $1.00.

For a firsthand look at this area's ethnic diversity, take a drive through downtown Paterson or a stroll up the aisles of **Corrado's Family Affair,** at 1578 Main Avenue in Clifton (973–340–0628). This huge, warehouse-style grocery store is jam-packed with foods from every nation: prosciuttos and mozzarellas, chayotes and tomatillos, kosher knishes, Afghani flatbread—and on, and on, and on.

Hudson/Newark Region

When American art began to claim serious critical attention in the early 1900s, a farsighted New Jersey collector and the remarkable institution he inspired were in the forefront of efforts to make works by American painters accessible to the public. The collector was William T. Evans, who in 1909 offered the town of Montclair twenty-six paintings on the condition that a museum be built to house them. The building request was met, and today the Evans collection forms the nucleus of *The Montclair Art Museum.* Opened in 1914, this was the first museum in New Jersey to be open to the public, and it remains one of the few institutions of its kind to limit its concentration entirely to American art—including an excellent collection of Native American art and artifacts.

Montclair was the home of the great landscape painter George Inness, and many of his most familiar works depict the Montclair environs. Most appropriately there are twelve Inness canvases in the museum's collection of more than a thousand paintings, watercolors, and other works. Also represented are such American luminaries as John Singleton Copley, Winslow Homer, Reginald Marsh, John Singer Sargent, Childe Hassam, Robert Henri, William Morris Hunt, and James McNeill Whistler. In addition the museum houses a 14,000-volume research library.

The Montclair Art Museum, 3 South Mountain Avenue, Montclair 07042, (973) 746–5555, is open Tuesday, Wednesday, Friday, and Saturday 11:00 A.M.–5:00 P.M.; Thursday and Sunday 1:00–5:00 P.M.; closed Monday and major holidays. Admission is $4.00 for adults; $2.00 for senior citizens; free for children under eighteen. The museum is free to all every Saturday.

What's in the Water?

*C*onnie Francis, Frankie Valli, Paul Simon, Whitney Houston, and Philip Roth all hail from Newark.

The Montclair Art Museum

In 1796 Israel Crane, at the age of twenty-two, constructed a turnpike that opened New Jersey's heartland to early trade; he also built a Federal-style mansion that was to become home to seven generations of his family. Today the *Israel Crane House* has been restored to look as it did between 1796 and 1840, and uniformed docents are on hand to provide a glimpse into life during that period.

On the premises are herb and pleasure gardens and an 1818 house, which has been converted into a country store and nineteenth-century post office.

The Israel Crane House, 110 Orange Road, Montclair 07042, (973) 744–1796, is open Sunday 2:00–5:00 P.M., mid-September to mid-June. Admission is $2.00 for adults, 50 cents for children. Group tours are available by reservation. Thanksgiving, Christmas, the Fourth of July, and the changing seasons are celebrated with traditional foods, music, and decorations. Call for details.

Eagle Rock County Reservation, just a half-mile from the Crane House, provides a magnificent view of the Manhattan skyline.

Authentically prepared food, reasonable prices, a casual atmosphere, and large portions explain the popularity of ***Mexicali Rose.*** This restaurant specializes in Mexican and Southwestern cuisine; house favorites include Shrimp Tequila, Tijuana Chicken, and fajitas. The restaurant, at 10 Park Street, Montclair 07042, (201) 746–9005, is open Monday through Saturday 11:30 A.M.–10:30 P.M., and Sunday noon–10:00 P.M.

If you happen to be in or around Montclair between the middle of May and early June, don't leave without visiting the National Historic Trust Site ***Presby Iris Gardens.*** These gardens are the legacy of Montclair citizen Frank H. Presby, a breeder of irises and a founder of the American Iris Society.

Having begun with a modest planting that included several of Presby's own iris hybrids, the gardens have grown to include more than 4,000 varieties—including some that date back to the 1500s. If you wish to refresh your memory of spring's iris pageant, return to Presby Gardens in September and October, when the *Remontant* (reblooming) irises come into bloom.

Admission to the Presby Iris Gardens, 474 Upper Mountain Avenue, Upper Montclair 07043, (201) 783–5974, and Mountainside Park, is free. The grounds are open in season from 10:00 A.M.–8:00 P.M. For information on times to see the iris displays, call the above number.

If you've ever thought about what it would be like to be an air traffic controller (but lack the tolerance for stress and superhuman doses of responsibility that go with it), head over to the *Aviation Hall of Fame and Museum of New Jersey* in Teterboro. Teterboro Airport, one of the nation's busiest facilities that serve private and commuter aircraft, needed a new control tower awhile back. Instead of tearing down the old one, though, authorities incorporated it into the Aviation Hall of Fame. Now, after looking over the Arthur Godfrey collection of aviation artifacts and watching films of historic events in New Jersey aviation history, visitors can head upstairs and witness takeoffs and landings from the same perch controllers used for years. There's even an audio hookup, broadcasting the directions that controllers in the new tower are giving to incoming pilots.

(The Arthur Godfrey connection with Teterboro, by the way, is both famous and infamous. One day the radio and television personality buzzed the tower in a fit of temper, and later he recalled the event in a song called "Teterboro Tower.")

The museum celebrated its twenty-fifth anniversary in 1997 by quadrupling the size of its Education Center adjacent to the new control tower. The building has a facsimile control tower; aircraft, helicopter, and rocket exhibits; and hands-on airplanes to "fly." New Jersey–built piston, jet, and rocket engines and a military aviation display dominate the Great Hall. There's a Hall of Fame, where exhibits present aviatrixes such as Amelia Earhart and Kathryn Sullivan (the first woman to walk in space), and astronaut Buzz Aldrin, a native New Jerseyan.

The Aviation Hall of Fame and Museum of New Jersey, Route 46, Teterboro 07608, (201) 288-6344, is open Tuesday through Sunday 10:00 A.M.–4:00 P.M. Admission is $5.00 for adults, $3.00 for senior citizens and children under twelve.

Teterboro sits on the fringes of a vast tract of land that was for centuries an uninhabited and virtually uninhabitable wilderness, even after populous cities and suburbs sprang up all around it. Variously called the Hackensack Meadows, the Secaucus Meadows, or simply the Meadowlands or Meadows, the marshy basin that surrounds the estuarial reaches of the Hackensack and Passaic Rivers constitutes a remarkable ecosystem that is, unfortunately, famous chiefly for the ways in which it has been abused over the past hundred years.

Construction of any magnitude was stymied because the Meadows' foundation consists of up to 200 feet of unconsolidated muck. Within recent memory railroads and their attendant structures were the only substantial fabricated works in the Hackensack Meadows.

In spite of this construction problem, people did find some uses for the Meadows, and the uses they found were responsible for the dubious reputation the area once carried. Thirty years ago, when you were driving on the turnpike through the Meadows on a hot summer day, you would roll up your windows (this was before auto air conditioning) when you got near Secaucus because of the stench of the pig farms that occupied the edges of the Meadows. And if it wasn't the pigs, it was the garbage—communities in North Jersey long ago took to using the Meadows as a giant solid-waste landfill. Finally, as if pigs and garbage weren't enough, there were all the jokes about missing mobsters who were spending eternity beneath the marsh grasses.

In the early 1970s everything started to change. Construction engineers figured out how to build on the Meadows' soil, and the Hackensack Meadows Development Commission (HMDC) was formed. The Meadowlands were zoned, divided, and conquered.

Fortunately the planners who undertook the development of the Meadows found room for the preservation of one of the more undisturbed tracts as the multiple-use *Richard DeKorte State Park.* It includes hiking and nature-observation trails as well as a miniwilderness wildlife-management area. For all the depredations of the past, the Meadows are still a fine place for birding. You can even borrow a pair of binoculars at the *HMDC Environmental Center,* where there are informative exhibits and a large, glassed-in wing that overlooks the wildlife-management areas.

The HMDC Environmental Center is located at the end of Valley Brook Avenue in Lyndhurst; take the Polito Avenue exit off Route 17 South. The center is open Monday through Friday 9:00 A.M.–5:00 P.M. and

Did You Know . . . ?

*I*t is believed that Snake Hill in the Hackensack Meadows is the eroded stump of an ancient volcano.

Saturday and Sunday 10:00 A.M.–3:00 P.M. The board-walk and trails are open daily, May through September, 8:30 A.M.–7:00 P.M.; October through March, 8:30 A.M.–4:00 P.M.; and April, 8:30 A.M.–6:00 P.M. Admission to the museum is $2.00 for adults; children under twelve, free. For more information call the center at (201) 460–8300.

For a historical perspective on the Meadowlands and environs, visit the **Meadowlands Museum** in Rutherford. This small institution, which is housed in a Dutch Colonial farmhouse, maintains files of historical photographs and documents that are available to researchers if not currently on display. In addition to the first-floor exhibits, which change three or four times a year, the museum also features reconstructions of colonial and turn-of-the-century kitchens on its lower level as well as exhibits of antique toys and dolls and New Jersey minerals on the second floor.

The Meadowlands Museum, 91 Crane Avenue, Rutherford 07070, (201) 935–1175, is open Sunday 2:00–4:00 P.M.; Monday and Wednesday 1:00–4:00 P.M.; and by appointment; closed August and on major holidays. A donation of $2.00 per adult and $1.00 per child is requested.

Head east now to the bluffs above the Hudson River at Weehawken. Known to motorists as the town on the New Jersey side of the Lincoln Tunnel, and to aficionados of Edward Hopper's paintings as the setting for his *East Wind over Weehawken,* this is where the career of Alexander Hamilton, the brilliant American statesman, Federalist papers writer, and first U.S.

secretary of the treasury, was cut short in a duel with Vice President Aaron Burr. Burr, who felt that his recent candidacy for the governorship of New York had failed largely because of the vociferous criticism of his old enemy Hamilton, made the formal demand for satisfaction; the two men met at what was then a secluded spot on the Jersey side of the Hudson on the morning of July 11, 1804. Pistols were the weapon of choice. Hamilton's shot missed; Burr's did not. The author of the Federalist papers died a day later, while Burr, his political career finished, left the area and began his descent into the shadows of American history.

The actual **Hamilton-Burr Duel Site,** which is marked today by a small park and a modest tablet, is on John F. Kennedy Boulevard East (also called by its old name, Hudson Boulevard East). Nearby is **Veterans' Memorial Park,** where there is a more impressive monument and bronze bust of Hamilton. Historical considerations aside, this is a particularly scenic spot at dusk on a late fall or winter afternoon, when lights twinkle on across the river in Manhattan.

If you've always wanted to visit the Ginza but haven't had a chance, plan a stop at **Yaohan Plaza,** a mall whose vendors specialize in Japanese (and other) goods. The centerpiece here is a giant market filled with exotic produce, fresh fish and noodles, and imported packaged goods. Go hungry .... The food concessions are a bit more eclectic than the shops, offering everything from sushi to kung pao chicken to Korean hot pot. The mall, at 595 River Road in Edgewater, (201) 941–9113, is open Sunday through Friday 9:30 A.M.– 8:00 P.M. and Saturday 9:30 A.M.–9:00 P.M.

Wood-grilled octopus salad and lamb shank wrapped in eggplant and baked in fresh tomato sauce are just two of Ersin Zeybek's specialties at the *Turkish Kitchen.* Working as a chef in his native Turkey, Mr. Zeybek perfected these and other signature dishes such as kabobs, fresh fish, and slow-roasted lamb. His wife, Sibel, greets guests at the door of the casual, fourteen-table restaurant. Bring your own alcohol, as there's no liquor license. Reservations are requested on weekends. The Turkish Kitchen, 3506 Park Avenue, Weehawken, (201) 863–1011, is open for dinner Tuesday through Sunday 5:00–11:00 P.M.

In 1915 Pope Benedict XV issued a plea for world peace, and the Reverend Joseph N. Grieff, pastor of Holy Family Church in Union Hill (now Union City), responded. He envisioned a production of an "Americanized" Passion play, modeled on the one presented every ten years since 1680 in Oberammergau, Bavaria. Thus began Union City's annual—and the country's oldest—Passion play. In 1931 the *Park Performing Arts Center* was built specifically for the Passion play, which is now performed here each Easter season. The 1,400-seat, Moorish-style

New Jersey Fast Facts

*N*ew Jersey . . .

- *is only four times larger than Rhode Island;*
- *has the highest population density in the country;*
- *is the birthplace of such entertainment luminaries as Bruce Springsteen, Jon BonJovi, Paul Simon, and the Chairman of the Board, Frank Sinatra.*

opera house now also hosts numerous other cultural events throughout the year.

The Passion play tells the story of the last days of Jesus as he preached, journeyed to Jerusalem, presided at the Last Supper, and was crucified. The play received an overhaul in 1985, when Father Kevin Ashe rewrote the script to alter the anti-Semitic reputation Passion plays have earned over the years. "The Park Theater's Passion play is an art form that teaches a lesson to Christians," Father Ashe states. "In times of social unrest, the play teaches us that we all come from the same roots. Christ himself was Jewish."

The center is at 560 Thirty-second Street, Union City 07087; call (201) 865–6980 for a schedule of events.

Union City has a large Hispanic population, so it's no surprise that some of New Jersey's best Latin restaurants and grocery stores are here. Mexican tortillas . . . Chilean empanadas (crusty turnovers) . . . Colombian batidos (a drink of whipped milk, fruit, and sugar)—the 3½-mile route along Bergenline Avenue running toward West New York is a Latin fresser's dream come true.

The 20,000-square-foot grocery store, Mi Bandera (518 Thirty-second Street off Bergenline Avenue), is a great place to stock up on provisions such as *molé* (a Mexican sauce made of chocolate and spices), and tomatillos. If you prefer to have the cooking done for you, the restaurant upstairs serves fabulous *chicharrones* (fried pork cracklings), *sancocho* (Cuban meat, yucca, and corn stew), and other Latin specialties. If you're in town on Saturday, stop at ***Celso's Cafe*** (4900 Bergenline Avenue)

for some delicious empanadas (beef, onion, and egg turnovers). Or stop in at *La Isla Cigars* (505 Forty-second Street off Bergenline Avenue), buy a hand-rolled cigar from Berto Ale, who learned his trade in Cuba, and meander up Bergenline smoking and grazing.

October of 1996 was a momentous month for steam-powered railroad enthusiasts as *Locomotive #614*, built at the Lima Locomotive Works in Lima, Ohio, in 1848, and restored by railroad enthusiast Ross E. Rowland, Jr., made its maiden voyage as a leader of a round-trip Fall Foliage Express from Hoboken, New Jersey, to Port Jervis, New York.

Built to pull the Chesapeake & Ohio Railroad's premier express passenger trains, the George Washington and the Fast Flying Virginian, between Richmond and Chicago over the eastern Continental Divide formed by the Allegheny Mountains, #614 was retired from service in 1952 and sat on a storage track in a Kentucky roundhouse for more than two decades. In 1976 she was overhauled and donated to the Baltimore & Ohio Railroad Museum in Baltimore. There she stayed until 1979, when Rowland, a crew of fifteen mechanics, and 100 volunteers commenced a rebuilding project that took eighteen months and $1.5 million.

The 434-ton, 16-foot-tall steam locomotive is scheduled to repeat its 180-mile foliage run each October. For information and/or reservations, contact Iron Horse Enterprises, Inc., 1 Railroad Avenue, Lebanon 08833; (908) 236–2299.

Since the early 1900s, passengers between trains have been walking the block from Hoboken's Erie-

Hoboken Terminal

*T*housands of workers take commuter trains in and out of Hoboken every day, but how many stop to take a look at the station? Built in 1907 for the Delaware, Lackawanna, and Western Railroad, Hoboken Terminal was one of the great transportation temples of the age. Much of the exterior—especially on the Hudson River facade where the DL&W ferries used to dock—is copper, its surface aged to a mellow green. Inside, the 90-by-100-foot main waiting room is lavishly decorated in limestone and bronze. The bilevel ferry concourse, no longer in use, once contained a restaurant with river-facing balcony, a sumptuous barbershop, and even an emergency hospital.

Out beneath the 607-foot train sheds, prosaic New Jersey Transit commuter cars now depart on short suburban runs—a far cry from the glory days, when crack overnight trains like the Phoebe Snow sallied out of Hoboken on their way to the cities of the Midwest.

Lackawanna Terminal to the **Clam Broth House** to down steamed clams and draft beer at the restaurant's bar. Those with a bit more time sit down to seafood platters, fried shrimp, and lobster. The restaurant is at 34 Newark Street, Hoboken 07030, (201) 659–2448. Open daily 11:00 A.M.–10:30 P.M.

Jersey City's **Afro-American Historical Society Museum** focuses on New Jersey's African-American people, places, and events, with changing as well as permanent exhibits. Among the latter: a 1930 kitchen reflecting the heart of an urban black home for that time and period; black dolls from the African Diaspora (some dating back more than 125 years); sculptures and paintings; and civil rights artifacts and collections of the 1950s and '60s.

In addition to exhibits, the museum hosts lectures and programs relating to the black experience, and each December the museum sponsors a Kwanzaa program. The New Jersey Afro-American Historical and Genealogical Society, Inc., meets at the museum on the second Saturday of each month at noon.

The Afro-American Historical Society Museum, 1841 John F. Kennedy Boulevard, Jersey City 07305, (201) 547–5262, is open Monday through Saturday 10:00 A.M.–5:00 P.M. Admission is free.

Whether or not you're a Jersey chauvinist who thinks the state flag should fly from Liberty's crown, it's nice to know that you can get out to Liberty Island and the **Statue of Liberty** without having to sail from the Battery. The Circle Line operates a ferry that leaves **Liberty State Park,** off exit 14B of the New Jersey Turnpike. The ferry operates frequently, but the times change with the seasons, so call ahead. It operates every day except Christmas. The fare is $7.00 for adults, $5.00 for senior citizens; and $3.00 for children ages three to seventeen. The best time to go is in the morning, before the crowds arrive. A parking fee is also charged. Call Liberty State Park at (201) 435–9499 for more information. For recorded schedule information, call (201) 915–3400.

The carhops are gone now, but little else at the **White Mana** has changed in fifty years. Dedicated patrons continue to pack the tiny, classic diner for the house

Katyn Memorial

*A*t Exchange Place, the busy centerpiece of Jersey City's revived business district along the Hudson River waterfront, stands one of the most stark and unsettling statues to ever commemorate a historic event. It is a standing soldier, his face frozen at the moment of death, impaled on a bayonet. The statue commemorates the execution of 11,000 Polish army officers by Soviet troops in the Katyn Forest during the spring of 1940. It serves as a reminder that Jersey City's considerable Polish population refuses to forget the betrayal, devastation, and slaughter that was the fate of their native land during World War II.

specialty, a grilled burger with onions on a soft bun, with pickle chips on the side (75 cents each). The key to the burgers' popularity? "The grill is saturated with onions, seasoned with onions . . . the more seasoned, the better burgers," says the day cook, Larry McMillan, who has been grilling Mana burgers for twenty-one years. The diner is at Manhattan and Tonnelle Avenues in Jersey City.

Newark, New Jersey's largest city, has two major troves of regional historical materials, the lesser known of which is the *New Jersey Historical Society.* This society is the repository of what has been called "an unparalleled collection of New Jerseyana," and the sheer bulk and diversity of its holdings support the claim. Here is a library of 80,000 volumes, open to the public for reference use, and a collection of 2,000 maps, 22,000 prints, and 1 million manuscripts, including the original New Jersey charter of 1664. The society owns 300 portrait and landscape paintings and thousands of drawings, as well as furnishings, silver, glass, and porcelain of New Jersey manufacture.

The New Jersey Historical Society, 52 Park Place, Newark 07102, (973) 483–3939, is open Tuesday through Saturday 10:00 A.M.–4:00 P.M. Admission is free.

The magnificent *Cathedral of the Sacred Heart* is a church of superlatives: It's the fifth-largest in the country, has the second-largest rose window in the United States (37 feet in diameter), and has the state's largest church organ. It's also considered by many to be the purest example of Classical French Gothic architecture in the Western Hemisphere. Organ recitals are given on alternate Sundays from September through April (admission $10), and tours of the cathedral are offered every second Sunday of the month or by appointment. The cathedral is open daily until 7:00 P.M. The National Historic Site is at 89 Ridge Street, Newark, (973) 484–4600.

Branch Brook Park is lovely at any time of the year, but magnificent in April when 2,700 Japanese cherry trees come into bloom. The park, at Franklin Avenue and Mill Street, Newark, is open year-round, dawn to dusk. Admission is free. For more information, call (973) 481–5302.

The 2,047-acre *South Mountain Reservation* is the most spectacular parkland in the greater Newark area. Covering parts of Millburn, Maplewood, and West Orange, South Mountain is maintained as a balanced mix of forest, meadows, bridle and bicycle paths, and

Sail Away

*F*ive state-owned marinas are administered by New Jersey's Park Service. They include Forked River State Marina in Forked River, (609) 693–5045; Fortescue State Marina in Fortescue, (609) 447–5115; Leonardo State Marina in Leonardo, (732) 291–1333; Liberty Landing Marina in Jersey City, (201) 985–8000; and Senator Frank S. Farley State Marina in Atlantic City, (609) 441–8482.

secluded hiking trails. From Washington Rock on the Crest Drive along the reservation's eastern border, there are magnificent views of the skylines of Newark and New York; on the Lenape Trail deep in the interior, it's possible to forget that there is any urbanization or even human settlement for miles.

Near the northern end of the South Mountain Reservation, on sixteen acres of land, sits **Turtle Back Zoo.** Northern New Jersey's largest zoo houses 500 animals of 200 different species, with an emphasis on animals originally found in New Jersey. The most recent exhibits have flight cages for the golden and bald eagles, and the gray wolves are presented in a naturalistic setting. More exotic animals include penguins, llamas, mouflon sheep, addaxes, and squirrel monkeys.

Admission includes the Turtle Back Railroad train ride through the scenic reservation (the train runs from March 15 through October, weather permitting), as well as access to picnic areas and the many special events featured throughout the year.

The zoo is at 560 Northfield Avenue, West Orange 07052, (973) 731–5800. Spring and summer hours are weekdays and Saturdays 10:00 A.M.–5:00 P.M. and Sundays 10:30 A.M.–6:00 P.M. In winter the zoo is closed weekdays during December, January, and February. On weekends the hours are 10:00 A.M.–4:30 P.M. unless icy conditions prevail. Admission from March 15 through October is $6.00 for adults, $2.50 for children ages two to twelve and senior citizens (ages sixty and over). Winter rates are $5.00 for adults and $2.00 for children.

Mention Thomas Alva Edison in the context of New Jersey, and chances are you'll be understood as referring to the great inventor's years at Menlo Park. Edison did, of course, have a home and laboratory in this little town near Rahway from 1876 to 1887, and it was here that he perfected the incandescent lamp, the phonograph, and the telephone transmitter. Edison is well remembered at Menlo Park, where there is a state park that bears his name. The house Edison lived in, however, is gone, and the workshop from which that first light bulb emerged has long since been removed to the Henry Ford Museum in Dearborn, Michigan. Fortunately a far greater collection of Edison memorabilia has been preserved at the **_Edison National Historic Site_** in West Orange.

West Orange is where Thomas Edison came to live and work following the Menlo Park years. Here is where he spent the last forty-five years of his life and where he developed the phonograph, movie camera, nickel-iron battery—the list goes on and on. More than one-half of the 1,093 Edison patents date from the West Orange years.

The Edison laboratories, which today form the core of

the national historic site, were the first modern research and development facility. In the opinion of many historians of technology, they represented the great man's most important contribution—the invention of a means of producing inventions; previously inventors had been men like the young Edison himself, tinkering in relative solitude. The West Orange labs showed that an organizational genius, with staff of sixty scientists and technicians, could turn out a succession of useful contrivances.

Guided tours of the Edison laboratories include the main building, which houses the original machine shops, stockrooms, and offices, including Edison's own library and office; the chemistry and physics labs; the powerhouse that once served the entire complex and now houses a museum; and a 1954 replica of the world's first motion picture studio—the "Black Maria" of 1893–1903.

Edison's house, Glenmont, is situated several blocks from the laboratories in Llewellyn Park. This twenty-nine room mansion was built in the Queen Anne style and is still furnished with many of the family's possessions. Thomas and Mina Edison are buried in a quiet corner of the gardens behind the house.

The Edison National Historic Site Visitor Center, Main Street and Lakeside Avenue, West Orange 07052, (973) 736–0550 is open daily, 9:00 A.M.–5:00 P.M. Access to the laboratory buildings and to Glenmont is only by guided tour. One-hour tours of the laboratory complex are offered daily, 10:30 A.M.–3:30 P.M. Thirty-minute tours of Glenmont are offered Wednesday through Sunday, 11:00 A.M.–4:00 P.M. Tours leave from the lobby of the

Memorabilia from a famous inventor's life are housed at
the Edison National Historic Site in West Orange.

Visitor Center. To be sure of getting a complete tour,
arrive before 2:30 P.M. An entrance fee of $2.00 is
charged for visitors over sixteen years of age.

Not to be outdone by Essex, nearby Union County has
also set aside some fine parklands. The best place to
head for a day's ramble hereabouts is the roughly 2,000-
acre *Watchung Reservation,* located between Summit
and Scotch Plains.

Although there are some cultivated rhododendron
plantings within the Watchung Reservation, most of the

Feltville

*A*n unexpected find amid the leafy glades of Summit's Watchung Reservation is the cluster of old wooden buildings that constitute the remains of the deserted village of Feltville. Feltville was the creation of New York businessman David Felt, who chose this site for a model paper-manufacturing and printing operation, complete with workers' housing. The place boomed from 1845 until about 1860, and has been a ghost town since 1880. Since then, the Reservation, a county park, has come to enclose the old industrial site.

land within its borders has been left as much as possible in its natural state. As at South Mountain, there are extensive hiking and bridle trails; for the hardy, a 10-mile loop called the Sierra Club Trail makes a circuit of the reservation, just within the boundaries.

Near the New Providence Road entrance to the Watchung Reservation is the ***Trailside Nature and Science Center,*** a well-run facility recommended to anyone who visits the park with children. In addition to exhibits on local animals, fossils, minerals, plants, and pond ecology, there is even a forty-seat planetarium. The center is open daily 1:00–5:00 P.M. For information contact Trailside, Coles Avenue and New Providence Road, Mountainside 07092, (908) 789–3670. Admission is free.

The setting for the ***Stage House Inn*** is old: a brick structure dating to 1737. But the food is definitely new—New American to be precise—and delicious. The cuisine calls for the blending of cooking methods and ingredients from numerous countries to create well-balanced American dishes, and chef David Drake does the job splendidly. Among his specialties: an appetizer of quail stuffed with lobster on a bed of lobster risotto garnished with sauteed chanterelles; a loin of veal entrée with celery root, caramelized apples, and smoky bacon; and glorious desserts such as apple tarte Tâtin. The restaurant, at 366 Park Avenue, Scotch Plains 07076, (908) 322–4224, is open for lunch Tuesday through Friday and opens at 4:00 P.M. for dinner Tuesday through Sunday.

You don't have to visit Vermont to show the kids where the syrup they're putting on their waffles comes from. Each February environmental scientists at the 16-acre ***Cora Hartshorn Arboretum and Bird Sanctuary*** tap the arboretum's sugar maples and boil up batches of delicious maple syrup. The process requires cold nights and warm days, so call ahead to find out when the sap is running and make a reservation ($5.00 per family). The wooded grounds at the Arboretum, at 324 Forest Drive, Short Hills, (973) 376–3587, are open year-round during daylight hours.

History of an abrupt and dramatic variety was made on the steps of Springfield's Presbyterian Church by its minister, the Reverend James Caldwell, during the Revolutionary War Battle of Springfield. As the battle raged over the fields, Continental troops ran out of the wadding that was used between powder and ball in the muzzle-loading muskets of the day. Caldwell, an ardent separatist and chaplain of one of the New Jersey regiments, dashed into the church and emerged with as many copies as he could carry of the then-standard Watts hymnbook. Tossing them to the soldiers at the foot

Heavy Stuff

*J*ersey City boasts two of the "world's biggest" of their kind: the largest concrete monument, a 365-ton fountain erected in 1911 at the main entrance to Lincoln Park; and the 2,200 pound Colgate Clock whose 50-foot face overlooks the Hudson River on Hudson Street.

of the church steps, the minister called out, "Give 'em Watts, boys. Put Watts into them." Many a Continental musket ball was seated atop a wadded page of hymns that day. Caldwell was minister of the **First Presbyterian Church** of Elizabeth from 1762 to 1781, when he was shot and killed. He preached with loaded pistols in the pulpit and kept a lookout in the belfry to warn of an approach of the British, who came on forays from Staten Island. The church building of Elizabeth was burned by the British and rebuilt in 1785–1787. The church burned again in an accidental fire in 1946, but the outer walls are the original 1787 structure. The inside was restored to its Colonial style and is an authentic representation of Georgian architecture. The adjacent graveyard represents an unbroken continuum of history that dates back to the late seventeenth century.

The church is on Broad Street and Caldwell Place, Elizabeth 07201, (908) 353–1518. The grounds are open daily during daylight hours; Sunday services are at 11:00 A.M. (10:00 A.M. in summer); Wednesday services are at noon. The church houses a museum and will be opened for visitors by appointment.

Far different, and more ancient, associations are suggested by a visit to Beth Israel Memorial Park, a Jewish cemetery in Woodbridge. Here are the **Bible Gardens of Israel,** conceived as a means of bringing the physical environment of the Holy Land to life in the New World. The vehicle used for this ambitious enterprise was horticulture; here are hundreds of the plants mentioned in the Bible, from olive, fig, and pomegranate trees to myrtle, oleander, and bay. The trees, shrubs, and flowering plants are arranged in four main gardens: The Garden of the Promised Land, the Garden of Moses, the Garden of Jerusalem (Garden of Peace), and the Garden of the Kings. Each individual specimen is identified by its Hebrew, English, and Linnean names.

In order to bring an added note of authenticity and significance to the biblical plantings, the garden's designers have incorporated boulders from Mount Canaan, Elath, and the River Jordan; stones from Aijalon, Galilee, and Mount Zion; and numerous other physical reminders of the land where the Scriptures were written. Artworks of marble, bronze, and wrought iron are tastefully integrated into the gardens.

The gardens, on Route 1 (near the Garden State Parkway), Woodbridge 07095, (732) 634–2100, are open daily during daylight hours. Admission is free.

PLACES TO STAY
IN THE URBAN NORTHEAST

GRAND SUMMIT HOTEL
570 Springfield Avenue East,
Summit 07901; (908) 273–3000;
fax (732) 473–4228

MARLBORO INN
334 Grove Street, Montclair
07042; (800) 446–6020 or
(201) 391–7700;
fax (201) 391–6648

PALACE HOTEL
2600 Tonnelle Avenue, North
Bergen 07047; (800) 548–4206 or
(201) 866–0400;
fax (201) 866–6007

ROBERT TREAT HOUSE
50 Park Place, Newark 07102;
(973) 622–1000 or
(800) 569–2300;
fax (973) 622–6410

WOODCLIFF LAKE HILTON
200 Tice Boulevard, Woodcliff
Lake 07675; (800) HILTONS or
(201) 391–3600; fax (201)
391–4572

WYNDHAM GARDEN HOTEL
21 Kingsbridge Road, Piscataway
08854; (732) 980–0400; fax (732)
980–0973

PLACES TO EAT
IN THE URBAN NORTHEAST

28
28 Church Street, Montclair;
(973) 744–9263

ARTHUR'S LANDING
Port Imperial at Pershing Circle,
Weehawken; (201) 867–0777

CAFE MATISSE
167 Park Avenue East,
Rutherford; (201) 935–2995

CHENGDU 46
1105 Route 46 East, Clifton;
(973) 777–8855; *(Chinese
cuisine)*

CHEZ MADELEINE
4 Bedford Avenue, Bergenfield;
(201) 384–7637

HIGHLAWN PAVILION
Eagle Rock Reservation, West
Orange; (973) 831–3463

LA SCALA
159 Fourteenth Street, Hoboken;
(201) 963–0884

THE MANOR
111 Prospect Avenue, West
Orange; (973) 731–2360

OFF THE BEATEN PATH

RESTAURANT NADIA
5 Highland Place, Maplewood;
(973) 763–3083

RESTAURANT JUNIPER
7 Ridge Road, Lyndhurst;
(201) 939–6019

RUTH'S CHRIS STEAK HOUSE
Lincoln Harbor, Weehawken;
(201) 863–5100

SADDLE RIVER INN
2 Barnstable Court, Saddle River;
(201) 825–4016

SONOMA GRILL
64 Hoboken Road, East
Rutherford; (201) 507–0043

SPIRITO GRILL
500 Harbor Boulevard, Lincoln
Harbor, Weehawken;
(201) 867–0101

STONY HILL INN
231 Polifly Road, Hackensack;
(201) 342–4085

THAI CHEF
664 Bloomfield Avenue,
Montclair; (973) 783–4994

OTHER ATTRACTIONS
IN THE URBAN NORTHEAST

**BOXWOOD HALL STATE
HISTORIC SITE**
1073 East Jersey Street, Elizabeth
07201; (973) 648–4540

**DR. WILLIAM ROBINSON
PLANTATION**
593 Madison Hill Road, Clark
07066; (732) 381–3081

FORT LEE HISTORIC PARK
Hudson Terrace, Fort Lee 07024;
(201) 461–1776

**GROVER CLEVELAND
BIRTHPLACE**
207 Bloomfield Avenue, East,
Caldwell 07006; (973) 226–1810

**HERMITAGE/JOHN
ROSENCRANTZ HOUSE**
335 North Franklin Turnpike,
Ho–Ho–Kus 07423;
(201) 445–8311

**HISTORIC NEW BRIDGE LANDING
PARK**
Main Street, River Edge 07661;
(201) 646–2780

LIBERTY SCIENCE CENTER
Liberty State Park, 251 Philip
Street, Jersey City 07305;
(973) 299–1000

**LONG POND IRONWORKS HISTORIC
DISTRICT**
West Milford; (973) 839–0128

46

NEW JERSEY CHILDREN'S MUSEUM
599 Industrial Avenue East,
Paramus 07652; (201) 262–5151

NEWARK MUSEUM
49 Washington Street, Newark
07101; (973) 596–6550

QUIETUDE GARDEN GALLERY
24 Fern Road, East Brunswick
08816; (732) 257–4340

**THOMAS E. EDISON MEMORIAL
TOWER AND MUSEUM**
Christie Street and Route 27,
Edison 08818; (732) 549–3299

Selected Regional Information Centers, Chambers of Commerce, and Visitor Centers in the Urban Northeast

Gateway Regional Tourism Council,
P.O. Box 602, Little Ferry 07643; (201) 641–7632

North Jersey Regional Chamber of Commerce,
*1033 Route 46E, Box 110, Clifton 07011;
(973) 470–9300*

Northern New Jersey and the Upper Delaware Valley

Not too long ago it was fair to state simply that the northwestern corner of New Jersey offered a marked contrast to the heavily urbanized communities to the east. Here were dairy farms, upland pastures, dense forests, and tucked-away lakes; between one small town and another, there was only a strip of two-lane blacktop and maybe an old-fashioned roadhouse with a pair of antlers over the bar.

Now things have gotten a little more complicated, and this part of New Jersey contrasts as sharply with itself as it does with any other portion of the state. The completion of I–80 in the 1960s opened the gates for the suburbanization of Sussex and northern Warren Counties; it's no longer unusual for someone to live out past Lake Hopatcong or up near Sparta and commute to a job in New York City. Dairy farmers have sold out by the score (the actual number of farms is up in Sussex, but acreage is down—the result of smaller specialty

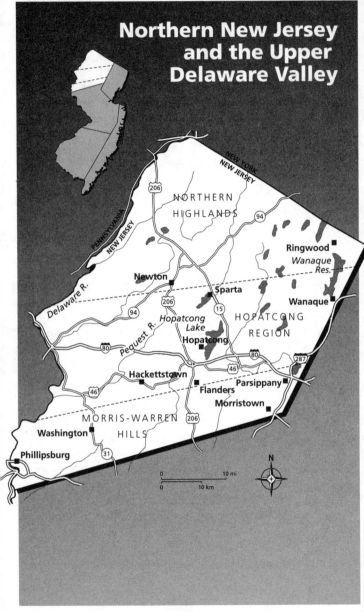

Northern New Jersey and the Upper Delaware Valley

NORTHERN NEW JERSEY AND THE UPPER DELAWARE VALLEY'S TOP PICKS

Peters Valley Craft Center

Walpack Inn

Carijon's Middleville Inn

Paulinskill Valley Trail

Franklin Mineral Museum and Mine Replica

Stokes State Forest

Space Farms Zoo and Museum

Van Bunschooten House

Ringwood Manor

Skylands Botanical Garden

Pine Hill Poultry Farms

Village of Waterloo

Black Forest Inn

Best's Fruit Farm

Picatinny Arsenal Museum

Pyramid Mountain Natural Historic Area

Four Sisters Winery

Pequest Trout Hatchery

Well-Sweep Herb Farm

Larison's Turkey Farm Inn

Fosterfields

Frelinghuysen Arboretum

Historic Speedwell

Craftsman Farms

operations that replaced dairying), and developers have moved in, building houses and pumping out press releases about the joys of living in "ruburbia," whatever that is.

Development tends to cluster along the major highways of northwestern New Jersey, and it still isn't hard to find a back road that will take you into a landscape more typical of the rural stretches of neighboring New York State and Pennsylvania. There are still beautiful country vistas along the Delaware River, from Phillipsburg north to High Point, and the most beautiful part of the upper Delaware Valley has wisely been preserved as the Delaware Water Gap National Recreation Area—a wonderful place for hiking (the Appalachian Trail parallels the river on the Jersey side) and canoeing. So don't write off Sussex and environs just yet. The suburban booster crowd may squeal with glee every time a new set of population projections for the year 2000 comes out, but it's a safe bet that there will still be plenty of open spaces to enjoy hereabouts for quite some time to come.

Note: This region is divided into three sections: the Northern Highlands, the Hopatcong Region, and the Morris-Warren Hills.

Northern Highlands

Hard upon the Delaware River, just north of the point where I–80 crosses into Pennsylvania, is a community devoted entirely to the perpetuation and teaching of fine craft. The **Peters Valley Craft Center** is a cluster of twenty-two buildings, thirteen of which are

AUTHORS' FAVORITE ATTRACTIONS IN NORTHERN NEW JERSEY AND THE UPPER DELAWARE VALLEY

Craftsman Farms
Fosterfields
Historic Speedwell
Ringwood Manor
Space Farms Zoo and Museum
Stokes State Forest
Well-Sweep Herb Farm

EVENTS IN NORTHERN NEW JERSEY AND THE UPPER DELAWARE VALLEY

Note: Schedules may vary; call ahead.

Warren County Heritage Festival, Oxford; May; (908) 453–4381

IBM/U.S. Equestrian Team Festival of Champions, Gladstone; June; (908) 234–1251

The Return to Beaver Creek Pow-Wow, Matarazzo Farms, Belvidere; July; (908) 475–3872

Quick Chek New Jersey Festival of Ballooning, Solberg Airport, Readington; July; (800) HOT–AIR–9

Sussex County Farm and Horse Show, Augusta; August; (973) 948–0500

Garden State Wine Growers' Fall Festival, Waterloo Village, Stanhope; September; (908) 475–3671

Civil War Weekend at Fosterfields, Morristown; October; (973) 326–7645

on the National Historic Register, but its importance to artisans throughout America far outweighs its size. One of only three dozen such communities in the country, Peters Valley offers intensive courses—with live-in accommodations—in blacksmithing, ceramics, fiber (basketry, paper and book arts, and surface design), fine metals, photography, weaving, and woodworking. Courses range from two to nine days, with basic to advanced instruction by nationally known artist/ teachers.

You don't have to be interested in actually learning a craft to come to Peters Valley; simple appreciation will do. Every Saturday and Sunday from June 1 through August 31, the studios are open between 2:00 and 5:00 P.M. so that visitors can watch resident craftspeople work and ask them questions. Evening slide lectures/presentations are held throughout the summer by workshop faculty and are open to the public free of charge. In addition the Peters Valley Craft Store and Gallery is well stocked with the work of a large group of American craftspeople, including the residents, and features changing displays and exhibits. The annual Craft Fair takes place during the last weekend in September. The fair includes more than 165 exhibitors, live music, food, and craft demonstrations. Peters Valley Craft Center is on Route 615, south of Layton (mailing address: 19 Kuhn Road, Layton 07851), (973) 948–5200. The store and gallery are open April through December. Call for hours.

"We feed the deer and people, too" is the motto of the folks at the *Walpack Inn.* They've been doing both since 1949. The deer come to within 20 feet of the restaurant to feed, and because the restaurant is a giant greenhouse (hundreds of plants are suspended from the ceiling), there are plenty of windows from which to watch the animals and enjoy views of the Kittatinny Ridge.

Hiking the Trail

*S*eventy miles of the Appalachian Trail, which stretches from Maine to Georgia, run through New Jersey. On the north the trail enters the state at Greenwood Lake, then follows the New York–New Jersey border west along the Kittatinny Ridge and continues to the Delaware Water Gap. Three-sided shelters and campsites are located at 8-to-12-mile intervals, at High Point State Park, Stokes State Forest, and Wawayanda State Park. Backpackers will find campsites at Worthington State Forest. Camping is allowed at the Delaware Water National Recreation Area. For information, call (973) 948–6500.

Friday night lobster and Saturday night prime rib are house specialties, as is Sunday brunch (11:00 A.M.–2:30 P.M.), which includes a raw seafood bar, omelet and waffle station, lots of hot entrées, fresh fruits, and desserts. There's a great salad bar and delicious home-baked loaves of Swedish bread. One might well imagine that the deer would rather be inside than out.

The restaurant, on Route 615, Walpack Center 07881, (973) 948–6505 or 948–9849, is open all year, serving dinner Friday and Saturday nights 5:00–10:00 P.M.; Sunday brunch 11:00 A.M.–2:30 P.M.; and Sunday dinner 4:00–9:00 P.M.

Although *Carijon's Middleville Inn* is about as off the beaten path as you can get in New Jersey, travelers and diners have been finding their way to this inn and former stagecoach stop in rural Sussex County for more than 200 years. The inn now functions strictly as a restaurant, and the menu is an eclectic mix of Italian and French, with a smattering of Cajun. Among the more unusual offerings: an appetizer of baked Portobello mushrooms with wild-mushroom fettuccine for $7.95; and an entrée of sautéed loin of veal medallions with pesto, roasted red peppers, and fontina cheese over pasta for $21. The restaurant is on Route 521 in Middleville 07855, (973) 383–9189. Lunch is served Tuesday through Saturday 11:30 A.M.–2:30 P.M.; dinner is served Tuesday through Thursday 5:00–9:00 P.M., Friday and Saturday 5:00–10:00 P.M.; Sunday brunch 11:00 A.M.–2:30 P.M.; and Sunday dinner 5:00–7:00 P.M.; closed Mondays.

Homemade soups and fresh-baked breads are house specials at the *Lafayette General Store & Eatery,* just off Route 15 on Meadow Road in Lafayette, (973) 383–7557. It's open daily for breakfast and lunch, 9:00 A.M.–5:00 P.M. A hearty meal should leave you well fortified for a leisurely stroll through *The Mill Antiques Center,* an 1850s gristmill, which houses the wares of forty dealers. Just off Route 15 in Lafayette, (973) 383–0065, it's open daily, except Tuesday and Wednesday, 10:00 A.M.–5:00 P.M.

At *Abbey Glen Pet Memorial Park,* 187 Route 94 South, Lafayette 07848, (800) 972–3118, Saint Francis of Assisi, patron saint of animals, watches over the "Hillside Burial" area. A special section of the fourteen-acre park is reserved for seeing-eye and therapy dogs, police canines and horses, and other animals who have dedicated their lives to public service. In the Country Burial area, pets' names are inscribed on a Gift of Love Plaque. The park is an inspiration to all animal lovers.

As the 26-mile *Paulinskill Valley Trail,* paralleling the Paulinskill River, winds through farm fields, rolling hills, woods, and swamps, it passes by nearly one quarter of New Jersey's plant species and offers spectacular views of the rural northwestern countryside. Once the bed for the Susquehanna and Western Railroad, the state's newest rail-trail passes by several old railroad-era buildings and still has whistle posts, mileage markers, and other relics from its railroad days. At milepost 89 (you're 89 miles from Jersey City), there's a great view of the Hainesburg Viaduct, considered the eighth wonder of the world when it was completed in 1911.

The trail endpoints are Brugler Road near Columbia and Sparta Junction. For information contact Rocky Gott, Park Superintendent, Kittatinny Valley State Park, P.O. Box 621, Andover 07821, (973) 786–6445.

It seems only fitting that getting to the state's last remaining glacial lake should require some effort. But knowing your effort is not going to go unrewarded counts for a lot. Forty-one acre, spring-fed *Sunfish Pond*, a designated National Landmark, lies in a chestnut oak forest high in the Kittatinny Mountains. It's a popular spot for hikers as well as migratory waterfowl and raptors.

Several steep and rocky paths lead to Sunfish Pond (called "hidden lake" by Native Americans). The trailhead for one of the most popular, the Appalachian Trail, begins at a parking lot just off I–80 (exit at the rest area/parking area for Dunnfield Creek). The 3.75-mile hike to the top passes through a hemlock forest and Dunnfield Creek Natural Area and then climbs to the pond.

For information on Sunfish Pond Natural Area contact Worthington State Forest, Old Mine Road, Delaware Water Gap, (908) 841–9575.

New Jersey's last operating zinc mine is now a National Historic Site. *Sterling Hill Mine & Museum* has more than thirty acres of exhibits, displays, and historical buildings. Those persons not suffering from claustrophobia will enjoy the underground mine tour, which winds through ⅕ mile of tunnel and passes by a spectacular mineral fluorescence display. The mine is at 30 Plant Street, Ogdensburg 07439, (973) 209–7212. It's open daily 10:00 A.M.–5:00 P.M. (last tour at 3:00 P.M.); closed December 1 through March 1. Admission is $8.00 for adults, $7.00 for seniors, and $5.00 for children under the age of seventeen (not recommended for children under six). A collection area is open to visitors the last Sunday of each month the mine is open. There is a charge of $10.00 to collect up to ten pounds of minerals, and an additional charge of $1.00 per pound for each pound over that amount. Collectors must be thirteen. Bring a jacket or sweater and good walking shoes.

There's a lot more than zinc in the north Jersey hills. The Franklin-Ogdensburg area of eastern Sussex County has yielded a greater number of species and varieties of minerals than any other location in the world—at last count, more than 340 species and 360 varieties. The Franklin minerals—the discovery of which was largely associated with nearly three centuries of zinc-mining operations that ended in 1954—are on exhibit at the *Franklin Mineral Museum and Mine Replica.* Franklin's rich mineral deposits are the result of a complex series of geological events that date back a billion years and were never duplicated elsewhere, hence the occurrence in local ore deposits not only of such an incredible diversity of minerals but of thirty types discovered nowhere else on Earth. For the layman perhaps the most interesting facet of the museum's display is the collection of fluorescent minerals—the world's largest—exhibited under ultraviolet light, which brings out their color and luminosity.

The mineral museum also includes a replica of the interior of a zinc mine, realistic to the last detail because it is made up of actual equipment used in the operations of the New Jersey Zinc Company in the days

We Called Him Uncle Guy

Old-timers living in the Upper Greenwood Lake area, near the border of Passaic and Sussex Counties, may remember a remarkably ingenious storekeeper named Guy Futrell. Arkansas-born, a one-time cowboy, and a chief petty officer in the U.S. Navy during World War I, Futrell came to Upper Greenwood Lake in the 1920s and built the first gas station in that then-wild region. His station, and the store he ran with his wife, Josephine, had Upper Greenwood Lake's first electric lights, run off a generator he built himself out of an old Model T. There was little Guy Futrell couldn't do, using his hands and his wits. In later life, he decided he'd like to make a violin. He read everything he could on the subject, then took a month just to fashion the necessary tools. Three months after that, he had two violins judged tonally near-perfect by a New York appraiser—a man who found it hard to believe that Futrell couldn't read a note of music.

—William Guy Scheller, Jr.

Did You Know . . . ?

• *The Rabbinical College of America, the world's largest institution for the study of Hasidic Judaism, is in Morristown.*

• *Reports of monsters in Lake Hopatcong, New Jersey's largest lake, date back to the seventeenth century.*

• *Roselle was the first city in the world to be lit by incandescent light bulbs.*

of active mining in the area. Under conditions such as those replicated here, miners discovered many of the rare and beautiful specimens on exhibit in the museum. Visitors can collect mineral specimens on the mine waste pile, adjacent to the museum, and test them for fluorescence.

Four relatively new rooms house exhibits of minerals from around the world, American Indian relics, fossils, and ongoing research.

The Franklin Mineral Museum and Mine Replica, Evans Street (off Route 23), Franklin 07416, (973) 827–3481, is open March 1 through December 1, Monday through Saturday 10:00 A.M.–4:00 P.M.; Sunday 12:30–4:30 P.M. Admission is $4.00 for adults, $2.00 for students to tour museum or collect minerals. To do both, fees are $7.00 for adults and $3.00 for children ages four to seventeen.

Stokes State Forest, which runs along 12 miles of the Kittatinny Mountain Ridge, offers some excellent hiking opportunities, including a 12½-mile section of the Appalachian Trail. For a particular treat, head over to the southwestern portion and hike to the "teacup" near the bottom of Tillman Ravine. The large pothole carved into rock at the bottom of the falls is a great place to kick back, soak your weary feet, and listen to the falling waters. The forest is 5 miles north of Branchville on U.S. 206, (973) 948–3820. The park office is open daily: Sunday through Thursday 9:00 A.M.–4:00 P.M.; Friday 9:00 A.M.–9:00 P.M.; and Saturday 9:00 A.M.–6:00 P.M. A parking fee is charged.

Gingerbread Castle is a northern New Jersey fairy-tale confection inhabited by lifelike storybook characters including Jack and Jill, Hansel and Gretel, and Humpty Dumpty. Tour guides relate the fairy tales or nursery rhymes associated with each of the figures, and a storyteller tells fairy tales in the open-air theater. The castle, on Route 23, Hamburg 07419, (973) 827–1617, is open daily except Mondays in summer months through Labor Day, 10:30 A.M.–5:00 P.M. Admission is charged.

As motoring families began to fan out along the nation's byways in the early years of the automotive age, an institution known as the "roadside attraction" came into existence. These attractions often took the form of small, randomly assembled zoos, many of which could still be found in the rural and suburban back roads of New Jersey as recently as twenty-five or thirty years ago. The vast majority of the roadside zoos fell victim either to development pressures or concern over the unprofessional way in which they were operated, but, fortunately, the best of the lot in New Jersey has continued to thrive: ***Space Farms Zoo and Museum,*** in Sussex, has operated for more than seventy years on a policy of clean surroundings, good care for animals, and public education.

Founded in 1927 by Ralph Space, Space Farms Zoo and Museum has grown under three successive generations of the Space family to comprise a 425-acre integrated operation. The zoo and museum cover 100 acres, and nearly all the remainder is used to grow food for the zoo's hooved animals and other herbivores. Of the land actually occupied by the zoo, as much as possible is maintained in natural-habitat condition.

Not that New Jersey is the natural habitat of all the creatures at Space Farms Zoo. There are, of course, white-tailed deer, foxes, raccoons, bobcats, black bears (more than a hundred are believed to roam wild in the state), snakes, and waterfowl indigenous to the area, but the Space collection also includes species such as lion, tiger, llama, yak, elk, jaguar, leopard, monkey, coatimundi, wolf, coyote, and mountain sheep.

An interesting adjunct to the zoo itself is the Space Farms museum complex, consisting of eight buildings that house an eclectic assortment of Americana: horse-drawn wagons and carriages, old cars and motorcycles, toys and dolls, Indian artifacts, firearms, and antique farm equipment.

Space Farms Zoo and Museum, Beemerville Road, Sussex 07461, (973) 875–5800, is open daily May 1 through October 31, 9:00 A.M.–6:00 P.M. Admission is $7.95 for adults, $3.50 for children ages three through twelve, and free for children under age three; group rates are available.

If present-day cities such as Paterson and Hackensack were little more than villages surrounded by farmland in the late eighteenth century, we can well imagine the

When Sussex County Was the Wild Frontier

*S*wartswood Lake, the lovely centerpiece of a state park just west of Newton, owes its name to an early Sussex County settler who died in what was likely one of New Jersey's last Indian attacks. Captain Anthony Swartwout was a British officer who had served in the French and Indian war, and who in 1756 was living with his family at a homestead near the lake. In that year a party of thirteen Indians, wartime enemies of Swartwout, raided his property and killed his wife. The captain shot several of the attackers but was soon captured, whereupon he was carted off and disemboweled by the Indians.

circumstances that prevailed in those days in the remote corners of Sussex County—and the hardiness of an individual such as the Reverend Elias Van Bunschooten, who was sent in 1785 by the New Jersey Synod of the Dutch Reformed Church to minister to the area's faithful. The Reverend Van Bunschooten built his Wantage Township farmhouse in 1787 and lived here until his death in 1815.

The *Van Bunschooten House,* recently restored by the local chapter of the Daughters of the American Revolution, contains furnishings and other artifacts characteristic not only of the minister's era but of that of later owners, the Cooper family, throughout the nineteenth century. Especially interesting is the contrast between the 1787 bedroom furnishings and the far more ponderous articles of 1860, exhibited in an adjacent room. Most important to the modern visitor, though, is the sense of perspective on time and distance that a place like this has to offer: same house, same location; 200 years ago an arduous trek from the Old Dutch towns along the Hudson, today a short scoot up Route 23.

The Elias Van Bunschooten House Museum, 1097 Route 23, Sussex 07461, (201) 875–3887, is open Thursdays and Saturdays 1:00–4:00 P.M., May 15 through October 15. For an appointment to visit on other days, call (973) 875–5335. A small donation is appreciated.

High Point State Park occupies more than 14,000 acres that touch the New York State border almost at the northernmost tip of New Jersey and also contains the state's highest peek, 1,803-foot High Point. High Point State Park represents a classic case of collaboration between private and public interest for the preservation of an outstanding natural area. Although the land that the park now occupies was part of a royal grant as far back as 1715, its remoteness assured that it would remain pristine throughout the following two centuries. The only construction of note was an exclusive resort, the High Point Inn, built in 1888 near the shore of Lake Marcia, which was remodeled into the present structure by the Kuser family of Bernardsville, New Jersey. In 1922 Col. Anthony Kuser made a gift of some 10,000 acres— the bulk of the modern park—to the state of New Jersey.

A multiuse park, High Point is managed with an eye toward balancing backcountry preservation with the provision of ample recreational facilities. The northernmost part of the park is the 800-acre John D. Kuser Natural area, much of which is old-growth Atlantic white cedar swamp. Just south of the natural area is the summit of High Point itself, topped with a 240-foot obelisk, which visitors may climb for

High Point State Park, named for the state's highest mountain peak, offers visitors both carefully tended nature preserves and modern recreational facilities.

spectacular views of the Delaware Valley, the Catskill and Pocono Mountains, and the lakes and forests of the park itself. (The monument, also a gift of the Kuser family, was completed in 1930.)

There are three public-access lakes within the boundaries of High Point State Park: twenty-acre Lake Marcia, at 1,600 feet the highest lake in New Jersey, has a supervised bathing beach; Lake Steenykill, west of Marcia, has a boat-launching ramp and two furnished cabins, which may be rented by family groups between

65

May 15 and October 15; Sawmill Lake, near the center of the park, also has boat-launch facilities (only electric motors are permitted on the state park's lakes), as well as fifty campsites.

Hiking is one of the prime attractions at High Point State Park. The Maine-to-Georgia Appalachian Trail runs north and south through the length of the park (look for white blazes) and is intersected by a system of nine park trails, varying in length from $1/2$ to 4 miles. Each trail is identified by blazes or markers of a different color, and relative difficulty is noted in a trail guide, available at the park office.

High Point State Park, 1480 Route 23, Sussex 07461 (located off Route 23, 8 miles north of Sussex), (201) 875–4800, is open daily throughout the year. Park entrance fees are charged from Memorial Day weekend through Labor Day; there is no entrance fee the rest of the year. A nominal amount is charged for the summit monument, and camping and cabin-rental fees are assessed.

Are you in the market for a limited-edition lithograph of Larry Bird? or Willie Mays? How about Louis Meyer? Pee Wee Reese? *Pelican Art Prints,* "The Sultan of Sports Art," has a huge selection at its sports-collectors' warehouse in Glenwood. These are lithographs of football, boxing, hockey, skiing, golf, and equine stars, as well as baseball and basketball pros and ace race-car drivers. All are individually hand-signed by the subject(s) and artists. The gallery is also a discount broker for state and federal duck prints. The gallery is at One Nasturtium Avenue in Glenwood 07418, (973) 764–7149, and is open daily.

Up along the New York State border, at the northern tip of Passaic County, is a state park rich in historical associations. ***Ringwood Manor,*** the focal point of ***Ringwood State Park,*** was established in 1740 and produced munitions for every major armed conflict from the French and Indian War to World War I. The Ringwood iron mines operated intermittently from the 1920s until 1957.

The present structures at Ringwood Manor reflect the period from 1854 to 1936, when the Hewitt family, who operated the mines under the auspices of Cooper Hewitt and Company, used the manor and its 33,000 surrounding acres as their country estate. The manor houses an excellent collection of furnishings, Hudson River School paintings, and prints and lithographs that reflect the tastes of patriarch Abram S. Hewitt and his family. In planning the gardens at the manor, Hewitt was inspired by the classical designs used for the grounds of the Palace of Versailles. Hewitt's son, Erskine, donated Ringwood Manor to the state in 1936.

In front of the manor are twenty-six links of an iron chain, which represents the West Point chain of 1778.

A visit to Ringwood Manor House is only part of the attraction of a visit to Ringwood State Park. The house is a fine place from which to head out onto a well-developed system of hiking and cross-country ski trails, some making a short loop on the immediate grounds and others heading northwest for a considerable distance into ***Abram S. Hewitt State Forest.*** (Detailed trail maps are available at the park office, in the Manor House.)

One recommended route takes you across the Ringwood River and Sloatsburg Road to Shepherd Lake (1½ miles), a nice place for swimming, fishing, and boating; it then extends another .8 mile to *Skylands Botanical Garden,* also part of Ringwood State Park, and formally called the New Jersey Botanical Garden at Skylands.

Skylands was sold in 1922 to Clarence McKenzie Lewis, an investment banker and trustee of the New York Botanical Garden. Determined to make Skylands a botanical showplace, he tore down the Stetson house and replaced it with a forty-four-room Tudor mansion (also of native granite), which features interior fixtures and architectural details imported from European chateaux and stately homes, as well as a fireplace piazza and an enormous room, used only for arranged cut flowers. He hired the most prominent landscape architects of his day to design the gardens and, for thirty years, collected plants from all over the world and from New Jersey roadsides. The result is one of the finest collections of plants in the state.

In March 1984 Governor Thomas Kean designated the ninety-six acres that surround the manor house as New Jersey's official botanical garden.

Ringwood State Park, off Route 511, Ringwood 07456, (973) 962–7031, is open daily all year from sunrise to sunset. Admission to the grounds is free, although a modest admission is charged for guided tours of the Ringwood Manor House and Skylands. Visitors should telephone in advance regarding schedules for tours of the houses.

"In our turbulent world so full of cross-currents, we have found a tiny haven; a place to give a demonstration of how life begins, continues, and, with the wonderful interaction developed eons of years ago, re-creates itself and goes on in peace and beauty." Thus May Weis described the 160-acre parcel of land in Ringwood that she and her husband, Walter, purchased in 1974 for the enjoyment of all. *The Weis Ecology Center* is a wonderful place to stroll or hike, observe nature, and learn about the northern New Jersey Highlands regions.

New Jersey Audubon Society's Weis Ecology Center, 150 Snake Den Road, Ringwood 07456, (973) 835–2160, is open Wednesday through Sunday 8:30 A.M.–4:30 P.M. The center also rents wooded campsites and rustic cabins by reservation only.

Hopatcong Region

The village of Hope, famous for its *Moravian Settlement,* founded in 1769 (call 908–459–5381 for information), is also home to *Pine Hill Poultry Farms.* The farm raises free-range chickens, which you can purchase fresh-dressed. Free tours of the farm are given daily, but call ahead. For those not interested in learning the fine details of the food they eat, there's a 1920s country store to poke around in. The farm is on Mt. Hermon Road, Hope 07844, (908) 459–5381.

Daylily aficionados will want to schedule a visit to Hemknoll Farm, one of (if not *the*) largest displayers of hybrid daylilies in the East. It offers a selection from more than 1,000 registered hybrids in all colors, sizes, bloom times, and heights. The gardens are in full bloom in July, but are lovely through August. Call ahead to schedule a visit. They're at 16 Great Meadows Road, Hope 07844, (908) 459–5778.

What do the Lenni-Lenape Indians, Bud Abbott, and Guy Lombardo have in common? At one time they all came to Lake Hopatcong, and they are all remembered at the *Lake Hopatcong Historical Society Museum*. Long after its first residents abandoned their hunting and fishing grounds, New Jersey's largest lake became a thriving resort, and celebrities such as Abbott and Lombardo summered here or were brought in to entertain guests.

Exhibits chronicle the lake's glory days—when bungalow colonies, fishing camps, and grand hotels circled the shore—and fun seekers flocked to the now-vanished Bertrand's Island Amusement Park, where Woody Allen shot *The Purple Rose of Cairo*. The museum amply chronicles the lake's golden age, an era that seems distant but was really only yesterday.

Lake Hopatcong Historical Society Museum, Lake Hopatcong State Park, (973) 398–2616, is open Sunday from noon to 4:00 P.M. from March through May and September through November. Admission is free.

The restored *Village of Waterloo* does a fine job of re-creating the character and physical environment of a bygone era—two eras, in fact: Waterloo was a lively town back in Revolutionary times, when local forges supplied armaments to Washington's troops, and it entered a whole new phase of growth and importance as a way station on the Morris Canal in the 1830s. The workaday world and domestic arrangements of both periods are brought to life here not only by the superbly restored homes, gardens, and commercial establishments open to visitors, but by working artisans and authentically costumed guides.

Restored and managed by the nonprofit Waterloo Foundation for the Arts, the village features a grist- and sawmill built in 1760 as a charcoal house; a blacksmith shop that still echoes with the clang of hammer on anvil; original towpaths of the 1831 Morris Canal; a general store that offers Waterloo-crafted textiles, pottery, wrought iron, candles, and brooms; and even a cozy tavern in which you can sit by the fire, have a tankard of ale, and pretend you are a jolly canal boatman, fortifying yourself against the elements. In all there are twenty-three restored houses and other structures on the property, including a number of antiques-furnished Victorian homes that reflect Waterloo's canal-era prosperity.

One of the newest additions here is an Indian village considered to be one of the most authentic reconstructions in the Northeast. The Lenape Village, on an island called Winakung (Place of Sassafras), faithfully re-creates the way of life of the Lenape (or Delaware) people who lived in this area more than 250 years ago.

Highlights of the village include a grove with symbols from a local Lenape petroglyph, a furnished bark longhouse whose interior replicates a trading session in 1625 between European traders and the Indians, and a native garden. There is also an Indian museum here, and a gift shop.

In addition to maintaining the village, the Waterloo Foundation each year sponsors the **Waterloo Festival for the Arts**, a May-to-October program of orchestral and chamber concerts, opera, jazz, and pop music. On Sunday afternoons concert tickets are included with admission to the village.

Waterloo Village, in Allamuchy State Park, Waterloo Road, Stanhope 07874, (973) 347–0900, is open daily except Mondays and Tuesdays. Mid-April until October, the village is open 10:00 A.M.–6:00 P.M.; October through mid-November, 10:00 A.M.–5:00 P.M. Closed mid-November through mid-April. Admission is $9.00 for adults, $8.00 for seniors, and $7.00 for children ages six through fifteen; under six, free. Weekend rates may be higher if a special event is being held.

The **Whistling Swan Inn**, a Victorian B&B in Stanhope, is "for those with more refined nesting instincts." Each of the ten rooms is furnished in a theme: Among them are an art deco room; an Oriental antiques room; a White Iron room; and a '40s Swing room. All the rooms have private baths—one with two claw-foot tubs in it. The inn is at 110 Main Street (P.O. Box 791), Stanhope 07874, (973) 347–6369.

Waiters and waitresses in Tyrolean costumes serve up German specialties as well as continental fare at the **Black Forest Inn,** recently chosen by readers of *New Jersey Monthly* as the best German/Swiss restaurant in the area. Portions tend to be large, the ambience Teutonic, and customers dress up to come to this multiroomed roadside inn at 249 Route 206, Stanhope 07874, (973) 347–3344. Open for lunch Monday and Wednesday through Friday as well as for dinner Monday and Wednesday through Saturday 11:30 A.M.–2:00 P.M., 5:00–10:00 P.M., and Sunday from 1:00–9:00 P.M.

The Wooden Duck B&B, right across from Kittatinny Valley State Park, offers privacy, comfortable accommodations, and, in the morning, lots of home-baked goodies. Set on seventeen acres of open fields and woodlands, the inn offers central air conditioning, a double hearth fireplace, game room, and swimming pool. Each of the five rooms has a queen-size bed, private bath, phone, TV, VCR, computer modem hookup, and writing desk. Those wishing ultimate privacy should request a room in the Horseless Carriage House. The inn is at 140 Goodale Road, Newton 07860, (973) 300–0395. Rates for a standard double range from $100 to $120.

Smell fresh-baked doughnuts? The aroma might well be wafting up from *Best's Fruit Farm* to the south. The folks at Best's have been baking doughnuts and pies and making apple cider for more than forty-five years, but the farm is most famous for its fruits and vegetables. The gourmet shop is a wonderful place to pick up all the fixin's for a picnic. The farm is on Route 46, just outside downtown Hackettstown, (908) 852–3777. The market/bakery is open year-round, Monday through Friday 9:00 A.M.–6:30 P.M., Saturday 9:00 A.M.–6:00 P.M. and Sunday 9:00 A.M.–5:00 P.M.

If you're in the market for some new spurs or a frock for the next square dance, continue west on Route 46 to the *Cherokee Trading Post* in Budd Lake. The store carries a complete line of Western apparel and boots, as well as moccasins and Indian crafts and jewelry. The store is open daily, year-round, 10:00 A.M.–6:00 P.M., and

Wednesday and Friday nights until 9:00 P.M.; (973) 347–1228.

Crossed Keys, built in 1790 as a working farm, is now an elegantly restored B&B with five working fireplaces, a fishing pond/ice-skating rink, a reflecting pool, and five guest rooms, each furnished differently. The Sconset room, with old, wide floorboards that have the original tilt to them, has a fireplace and overlooks the gardens and meadows; the Victorian Suite has a private sitting area and is furnished with Victorian antiques. The inn is at 289 Pequest Road, Andover 07821, (973) 786–6661.

Just north of Route 80 near Dover, the U.S. Army maintains an armament research, development, and engineering center known as the Picatinny Arsenal. Here is a highly specialized and little-known facility, the ***Picatinny Arsenal Museum,*** housing the most extensive collection of ordnance you are ever likely to come across: ammunition, bombs, small arms, rockets, mortars, grenades, booby traps, and similar military hardware. There is an impressive historical and geographical breadth to the museum's exhibits. American items range from forge equipment, used to make cannonballs for the Continental army in the Revolution, to the Patriot missile warhead used in Operation Desert Storm. Foreign hardware from both world wars, Korea, and Vietnam is also displayed.

The Picatinny Arsenal Museum, off Route 15, Picatinny Arsenal 07806, (973) 724–2797, is open Tuesday to Thursday 9:00 A.M.–3:00 P.M. or by appointment. The museum is closed from Christmas to New Year's and when the arsenal is closed. Admission is free.

During the last Ice Age, the Wisconsin Glacier passed through northern New Jersey and deposited strange, massive boulders, called "erratics" by geologists. Some historians believe that Tripod Rock on Pyramid Mountain was a sacred place for the Lenni-Lenape people, and that two smaller boulders nearby were used as a calender by early inhabitants. The 243-ton boulder was deposited by the Wisconsin glacier more than ten thousand years ago.

There is no doubt that the 1,000-acre **Pyramid Mountain Natural Historic Area** is an excellent place for hikers and nature lovers. Rugged hills, kettle holes, and streams are home to more than 400 species of plants and wildflowers, 100 species of birds, and 30 species of mammals.

Six main hiking trails, each blazed with a different color, traverse the north/south axis of the area. Follow the white trail to Tripod Rock, which perches precariously on three smaller boulders and is one of numerous glacial erratics in the park. Nearby Bear Rock (white/blue trail) is one of the largest in the state. The Pyramid Mountain Visitors Center, 472A Boonton Avenue, Boonton, (973) 334–3130, is open Friday through Sunday 10:00 A.M.–4:30 P.M. Trails are open year-round from sunrise to sunset. To get to Pyramid Mountain Natural Historic Area from I–287, take exit 44A at Main Street in Boonton. Turn right on Boonton Avenue (County Route 511) and head north 4 miles to the entrance, on the left.

The oldest Storyland park in Northern New Jersey—thrilling kids since 1957—recently underwent a name change and a face-lift. The former Fairy Tale Forest is now *Hot Diggity's at Fairy Tale Forest*, but little else has changed other than some major spiffing up. The children's village, based upon fairy-tale characters and settings and built virtually single-handedly by German immigrant Paul Woehle, has been taken over by his granddaughter, who is dedicated to maintaining the same attention to detail her grandfather did.

The twenty-acre park is dotted with the abodes of Hansel and Gretel, Rapunzel, the Gingerbread Boy, Rumpelstiltskin, Cinderella, Snow White and the Seven Dwarfs, and many other favorites from Hans Christian Andersen and the Brothers Grimm. Each site features a building with a life-size tableau; some, like the three-ring circus and toy workshop, are mechanically animated. Kids love to ride the antique, twenty-four-horse carousel and fire engine and curl up in Mother Goose's giant nest and listen to stories. Of all the "C'mon, let's stop here!" places scattered along America's roads, this is one of the most imaginative and worthwhile for kids up to the age of seven or eight.

Hot Diggity's at Fairy Tale Forest, 140 Oak Ridge Road, Oak Ridge 07438, (973) 697–5656, is open April through December. Call ahead for days and hours. Admission is $6.00 adults; $5.00 for children ages two to twelve, under two, free. Parking is free. There is a snack bar in the park.

Enjoy a picnic lunch while you take in some history at *Washington Rock State Park*. From the rock promontory here, General George Washington was able to see for 30 miles, enabling him to plot a maneuver that brought his troops behind those of British General William Howe, blocking the enemy's retreat. The fifty-one-acre park, with picnic tables and grills, is on top of Watchung Mountain in Green Brook Township. For information call (201) 915–3401.

Did you know that when a baby ostrich is born it weighs about three pounds? Or that ostriches take three years to reach maturity? Or that when they're scared, rather than sticking their heads in the sand, they can run up to 55 miles per hour? Or that the ungainly African birds make the *Flower Place* one of New Jersey's most unusual family attractions?

At the Flower Place, the ostriches are outside in pens, while a rainbow palette of fresh flower arrangements are artfully displayed inside the 1865 barn, which is also chock-full of baskets as well as figurines made by proprietor Jun A. Omata from natural materials such as dried leaves, twigs, feathers, wood bark, and mushrooms. Upstairs the walls are decorated with tapestries as well as original paintings by resident artist, R. D. Walker; and there's a fine collection of Oriental antiques and art and hand-crafted silver jewelry.

The Flower Place, 53 Sarepta Road, Belvidere, (908) 475–1446, is open Wednesday through Sunday 9:00 A.M. to 6:00 P.M.

Any time of the year is a good time to visit *Matarazzo Farms,* but in fall, when you can pick your own pumpkins and apples and sample the fresh-pressed apple cider, the 392-acre farm is extra special. *Four Sisters Winery,* on the grounds of the farm, gives free tastings all year and complimentary tours on weekends. If you really like getting into the act, ask the winery

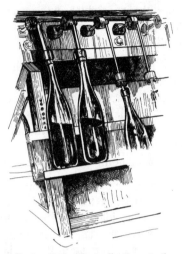

The Four Sisters Winery offers tours, tastings,
and even grape stomping.

about its grape-stomping parties. The farm and winery
are on Route 519, 10 Doe Hollow Lane, Belvidere 07823.
For information on the market, call (908) 475–3671.

If you've ever wondered about the origins of those
hatchery trout you fish for in spring, a visit to the
Pequest Trout Hatchery should answer all your
questions. The Pequest facility, located 9 miles west of
Hackettstown, has, since its opening in 1982, produced
more than 600,000 brook, brown, and rainbow trout per
year for distribution in New Jersey's lakes and streams.
It takes eighteen months for the hatchery to raise a fish
to stocking size, and the job involves careful maintenance of water temperature and aeration, feeding, and
disease-prevention measures. The early stages of the

operation, in which brood fish spawn and eggs are incubated and hatched, are conducted in closed quarters inaccessible to visitors, but anyone can watch the growing trout through windows in the nursery building and in the mile of outdoor concrete raceways on the Pequest premises.

Also on the hatchery grounds is the ***Pequest Natural Resource Education Center,*** housing exhibits that explain riverine ecology, with specific emphasis on the life cycle of trout—including a display tank that approximates a cross-section of a typical trout stream. Videos and self-guided tours of the hatchery complete the educational experience. Special programs are offered year-round and are listed in the center's *Budding Naturalist* brochure.

The Pequest Trout Hatchery, off Route 46 near I–80 (exit 19), Oxford 07863, (908) 637– 4125, is open daily except holidays, throughout the year, 10:00 A.M.–4:00 P.M. Admission is free.

From ashwaganda to yucca, ***Well-Sweep Herb Farm*** showcases and sells one of the largest selections of herbs in the country, exhibiting them along with a large collection of perennials in a natural setting. There's also a formal educational display herb garden, as well as medicinal, perennial, English cottage, rock, and vegetable gardens. Among the herb selection: 36 types of basils, 60 different lavenders, 80 varieties of thyme, and 100 varieties of scented geraniums. The biggest selection—when weather cooperates—is available around May 15, but there's lots to see and buy year-round, and the fields, with flowers drying, are particularly magnificent during July and August.

Well-Sweep Herb Farm, 205 Mt. Bethel Road, Port Murray 07865, (908) 852–5390, is open Monday 1:00–5:00 P.M., Tuesday through Saturday 9:30 A.M.–5:00 P.M.; closed Sundays and holidays. From January through March, call ahead to make sure they'll be open.

Morris-Warren Hills

The gracious 1770s *Stewart Inn* is a stone manor house on sixteen acres of lawns, woods, stream, and pasture. There are a swimming pool, trout stream, barn, outbuildings, and farm animals. A full breakfast is included in the B&B's rates, which run from $95 to $125 per night, double occupancy. The inn is on South Main Street (mailing address: Box 571, R.D. 1), Stewartsville 08886, (908) 479–6060.

Since the early 1700s the town of Chester has been a magnet for travelers. The first white settlers established farms and shops on the Black River, along paths the native Lenni-Lenape had carved out. By 1771 a weekly stagecoach ran from Jersey City to Chester's (then known as Black River) Crossroads. In the early 1800s the road was improved: Washington Turnpike (Route 240) ran through town, and the Brick Hotel opened to serve weary travelers.

Chester really became a boomtown in 1867, when iron ore was discovered along Main Street. Unfortunately, twenty-five years later, the ore ran out, and Chester quickly became a ghost town. In the 1950s a local family opened a restaurant at The Crossroads (which had been moved west a quarter of a mile with the cutting of Route 206). They launched a major advertising campaign,

A Forgotten Canal

*M*uch of the Delaware and Raritan Canal, which slices
across the Garden State at its narrowest part, has been
preserved as a park waterway. But the more northerly Morris
Canal, which once had its western terminus at Phillipsburg, is
gone and largely forgotten.

*The Morris Canal reached from Newark Bay to the Delaware
River, ascending from sea level to an altitude of 914 feet at Lake
Hopatcong, then dropping to 760 feet at the Delaware—all via
a system of twenty-three inclined planes. Completed in 1831 at
a cost of nearly $3 million, it could accommodate canal boats
weighing up to twenty-five tons. But like many other waterways
dug during America's golden age of canal building, the Morris
Canal soon fell prey to competition from the newer and faster
railroads. The Lehigh Valley Railroad leased the canal in 1871
and prevailed upon the state to take it over in 1903. Twenty-one
years later it was destroyed, by state order.*

inviting travelers to dine in one of the town's oldest
buildings, and the tourists once again started coming to
Chester. Today the folks at ***Larison's Turkey Farm Inn***
continue to serve up family-style, all-you-can-eat turkey
dinners, and travelers continue to flock to the early-
nineteenth-century, antiques-filled farmhouse/restaurant.
Steak, ham, and fish are also on the menu. The inn, at the
intersections of routes 206 and 24, Chester 07930, (201)
879–5521, is open daily 11:00 A.M.–9:00 P.M.

As tourists began to return to Chester, residents opened
shops along the historic Main Street to attract more
tourists. They *were* attracted, and today downtown
Chester is thriving. Baseball fans may want to pause for a

moment in front of the **Emporium Shop** at 71 Main Street. The house was once home to Billie Dee's Store, which sold newspapers and candy. Billie Dee was also a baseball pitcher and is credited with having invented the curveball when his finger got caught in the covering of a ball. **Taylor's Ice Cream Parlor,** in the 1876 Centennial Building, is a great place for a light snack. The Brick House is now the **Publick House** and still rents rooms and serves lunch and dinner daily. Call (908) 879–4800.

If you've a hankering for a hot steak and a cold beer, swing by **Jersey Jim's Brewing Company**. Pale ale, oatmeal stout, amber, black and tan ... they're all brewed right here, 540 gallons at a time. Proprietor Jim Richards will be happy to show you just how he turns malt, yeast, water, and hops into one of humankind's oldest companions. The restaurant/brewery is at 150 Route 206 in Hillsborough, (908) 526–5584.

Before you head toward Morristown, go a mile in the other direction on Route 24 (toward Long Valley) to visit **Cooper Mill,** one of the few waterpowered mills still operating in New Jersey. Built in 1826 on the site of a pre-Revolutionary mill, it was restored in the 1970s by the Morris County Park System. For information write to P.O. Box 1295, Chester 07930, or call (973) 326–7646. The mill is open for tours weekends in May, June, September, and October 10:00 A.M.–5:00 P.M. (the last tour leaves at 4:00 P.M.). In July and August it's open Friday through Tuesday 10:00 A.M.–5:00 P.M. A donation of $3.00 for adults and $2.00 for children is requested.

Heading back east we come to Morristown, perhaps best known to visitors for its national historic site that relates to the Continental army's encampments in

1776–77 and 1779–80. The two centuries that have passed since Washington and his men camped here have seen the surrounding countryside change from farms to still-growing suburbs, with one important exception. This is *Fosterfields,* a "living historical farm" maintained as an example of what agriculture was like in New Jersey one hundred years ago.

The 200-acre tract that became Fosterfields had been cultivated for a century or more by 1852, when Paul Revere's grandson, Lieutenant Joseph Warren Revere, bought the land and built his country seat, The Willows, here. There have been only two private owners of Fosterfields since Revere: Charles Foster, who bought the property in 1881, and his daughter, Caroline Rose Foster, who inherited it in 1927 and lived here until her death in 1979 at the age of 102. Near the end of her long life, Miss Foster donated her farm to the Morris County Park Commission, which maintains it, using much the same farming techniques her father employed in the late 1800s. Everything is authentic—tools, plows, and harvesting equipment, and, of course, the horses that turned the wheels of farms and much of civilization itself four generations ago.

In addition to following the self-guided trail through the farm or taking one of the guided tours offered on Sundays at 2:30 P.M., visitors to Fosterfields are encouraged to participate in a busy schedule of workshops and demonstrations that emphasize old-time agricultural, crafts, and home-economics techniques. The Willows, the Gothic Revival mansion on the site, is open for tours April through October, Thursday through Sunday, 1:00–4:00 P.M.

Fosterfields, Route 24 and Kahdena Road, Morris Township 07962, (973) 326–7645, is open April through October, Wednesday through Saturday (and holidays), 10:00 A.M.-5:00 P.M.; Sunday, noon-5:00 P.M. Admission is $4.00 for adults, $3.00 for seniors, and $2.00 for children ages six through sixteen. Under six, free. There is an additional $1.00 charge to visit The Willows.

Another gem of the Morris County Park Commission is the *Frelinghuysen Arboretum,* surrounding the stately Colonial Revival mansion that houses the commission's offices. All the trees in the arboretum are identified by species, and among the numerous trails that crisscross the property is a natural path for the blind, with signs in braille. The Frelinghuysen Arboretum is especially beautiful in springtime, when azaleas, rhododendrons, roses, and spring bulb plants bloom in profusion, but cross-country skiers should also keep the trails in mind for fine winter sport.

The Frelinghuysen Arboretum, on East Hanover Avenue near Whippany Road, Morris Township 07962, (973) 326–7600, is open daily during daylight hours; closed Thanksgiving, Christmas, and New Year's days. Admission is free.

Historic Speedwell recalls the lives and work of a family that played an important part in the transformation of the United States from an agricultural to an industrial nation in the nineteenth century. Stephen Vail was the owner of the thriving Speedwell Iron Works, a cast-iron foundry powered by the fast-running Whippany River. One of the most important commissions of the Speedwell works in the early 1800s was for the iron

The first message transmitted by "Morse code" was sent years before Morse's more famous "What hath God wrought."

machinery used in the SS *Savannah,* the first steamship to cross the Atlantic Ocean.

While attending New York University, Vail's son, Alfred, met Samuel F. B. Morse, who had come to demonstrate a rudimentary apparatus he had devised for sending electromagnetically generated signals over wires. Alfred offered Morse financial backing and helped perfect the device at Speedwell. On January 6 Alfred sent the first message, "A patient waiter is no loser," on a working model of the improved telegraph. The more famous "first" telegraph message, Morse's own "What hath God wrought," was transmitted to Vail at Baltimore six years later over an improved apparatus featuring a register that recorded the dots and dashes of Morse code on a strip of paper. The machinery, too, was built by Vail at Speedwell.

Today, Speedwell enjoys designation as a National Historic Site. Structures open to visitors at Speedwell include Vail House itself, restored to its 1840s appearance; the 1829 building where the first public demonstration of the telegraph was made on January 11, 1838; and the granary, housing exhibits of antique tools and vehicles. In addition to these original structures, the Speedwell property is the site of three eighteenth- and early-nineteenth-century houses moved here from Morristown in the 1960s.

Historic Speedwell, 333 Speedwell Avenue, Morristown 07960, (973) 540–0211, is open to the public and for group tours during the warm weather months. Call for dates and hours. Admission is $5.00 for adults, $2.00 for senior citizens, and $1.00 for children ages six through sixteen.

If you don't mind using your feet to get off the beaten path, *Morris County* offers some excellent options.

The Farney Highlands Trail system in Jefferson and Rockaway townships encompasses the Four Birds Trail, an isolated, 19.4-mile segment that crosses only one paved road. The four birds refer to environments found along the trail: wild turkey in the forests; red-tailed hawk near the cliffs; osprey on the shores of the lake; and, in the marshes, great blue heron. The trail is a great place for migratory bird-watching in the fall. To reach the southern trail head, take Route 513 north from Route 80 in Rockaway Township, and, after 2.75 miles, turn right onto Sunnyside Road. Look for white blazes about 150 feet down on the left. The northern section of the trail is on land owned by the Newark Watershed Conservation and Development Cooperation. Call (973) 697–2850 for a hiking and parking permit.

Fort Nonsense

*M*orristown is rich in relics of the days when New Jersey was the "Cockpit of the Revolution." On the grounds of Morristown National Historical Park are the Ford Mansion, twice Washington's winter headquarters, and the site of the troop encampment at Jockey Hollow. A lesser known Revolutionary War site on the park's grounds is Fort Nonsense, marked by an earthworks reconstruction on Morristown's Mount Kemble. Why the irreverent name? The fort, constructed in 1777 under George Washington's orders, was never used except for storage of supplies. As the years wore on, locals came to suspect that the Commander had built it only to keep his men busy during a long winter bivouac. So they named it Fort Nonsense, in what was perhaps the only instance of that word being connected with the decidedly no-nonsense Father of His Country.

Head over to Morris County's **Mount Hope Historical Park** to see remains of the county's twentieth-century iron mines. Pick up a trail guide at the parking lot and then meander along 3 miles of trails that wind past historic sites, including numerous subsidence pits (large holes created by abandoned mine shafts). Keep an eye open for chunks of magnetite iron ore—small, black, somewhat rectangular rocks. To reach the park, take I–80 to exit 35 north towards Mount Hope. After .5 mile, turn left onto Richard Mine Road, then turn right onto Coburn Road after .7 mile. When the name of the road changes to Teabo Road, watch for the parking lot after another .7 mile.

For maps and information on all of Morris County's parks, call (973) 326–7600 weekdays. Maps are available at the Hagarty Education Center at the Freling-huysen Arboretum.

Gustav Stickley, the foremost American spokesperson for the Arts & Crafts Movement, was a proponent of "a fine plainness" in art and the art of living. He incorporated his philosophy of building in harmony with the environment by using natural materials when he built his log home at *Craftsman Farms* circa 1908–1910. As he explained in his magazine, *The Craftsman*, in November 1911: "There are elements of intrinsic beauty in the simplification of a house built on the log cabin idea. First, there is the bare beauty of the logs themselves with their long lines and firm curves. Then there is the open charm felt of the structural features which are not hidden under plaster and ornament, but are clearly revealed, a charm felt in Japanese architecture ... The quiet rhythmic monotone of the wall of logs fills one with the rustic peace of a secluded nook in the woods."

Stickley dreamed of establishing a farm school for boys at his "Garden of Eden," but his dream began to fade as the tastes of the American people moved away from the clean, strong lines of Craftsman furniture toward revival of early American and other styles. The dream died in 1915, when he filed for bankruptcy. In spite of these failures, he was a visionary, whose philosophy of art and architecture helped people make the transition from the overwrought interiors of the Victorian Age to the modern decorative arts to come.

The Log House at Craftsman Farms is a National Historic Landmark.

Twenty-six acres of the 650-acre tract that originally made up Craftsman Farms have been declared a National Historic Landmark. The landmark is owned by the Township of Parsippany-Troy Hills and is operated by The Craftsman Farms Foundation, which is restoring the interior of the house and the gardens as they were in Stickley's time. Many of his original pieces of Mission furniture and comparable period Stickley pieces are on display to show how the house would have looked in his day.

The interior of the Main Log House at Craftsman Farms, on Route 10-W and Manor Lane, Parsippany (mailing address: Box 5, Morris Plains 07950), (973) 540–1165, is open April through October on Thursdays noon–3:00 P.M.; and Saturdays and Sundays 1:00–4:00 P.M. (The last tour starts at 3:15 P.M.) Throughout the season there are a variety of special events, including Sunday "Chats in the Garden" and a crafts fair. Call for a calendar.

PLACES TO STAY
IN NORTHERN NEW JERSEY
AND THE UPPER DELAWARE
VALLEY

THE BERNARDS INN
27 Mine Brook Road,
Bernardsville 07924;
(888) 766-0002 or
(908) 766-0002;
fax (908) 766-4604

CHESTNUT HILL ON THE DELAWARE
63 Church Street, P.O. Box N,
Milford 08848; (908) 995-9761

INN AT MILLRACE POND
313 Johnsonburg Road, Box 359,
Hope 07844; (800) 746-6467 or
(908) 459-4884;
fax (908) 459-5276

INN AT PANTHER VALLEY
Route 517, Box 183, Allamuchy
07820; (908) 852-6000;
fax (908) 850-1503

OLDE MILL INN
225 Route 202, exit 30B (Route
287), Basking Ridge 07920;
(800) 585-4461 or
(908) 221-1100;
fax (908) 221-1560

SOMERSET HILLS HOTEL
200 Liberty Corner Road, Warren
07059; (908) 647-6700

WHISTLING SWAN INN
110 Main Street, Stanhope 07874;
(973) 347-6369

THE WOOLVERTON INN
6 Woolverton Road, Stockton
08559; (888) AN-INN-4U or
(609) 397-0802;
fax (609) 397-4936

PLACES TO EAT
IN NORTHERN NEW JERSEY
AND THE UPPER DELAWARE
VALLEY

BLACK FOREST INN
249 Route 206, Stanhope;
(973) 347-3344
(German and Continental
cuisine)

CHRISTINE'S
Somerset Hills Hotel, 200 Liberty
Corner Road, Warren;
(908) 647-6700

CULINARY RENAISSANCE
12 Center Street, Metuchen;
(973) 548-9202

IL CAPRICCIO
633 Route 10, Whippany;
(973) 884-9175

KIKI RIOS
1316 Route 31 North, Annandale;
(908) 735–6700
(Southwestern/Mexican cuisine)

LA VIET
129 East Front Street, Plainfield;
(908) 668–8080
(Vietnamese cuisine)

PERRYVILLE INN
113 Perryville Road, Hampton;
(908) 730–9500

SCALINI FEDELI
63 Main Street, Chatham;
(973) 701–9200

VENEZIA RISTORANTE
Chester Springs Shopping Center,
Route 206, North Chester;
(908) 879–2848

OTHER ATTRACTIONS
IN NORTHERN NEW JERSEY AND THE UPPER DELAWARE VALLEY

ACORN HALL
68 Morris Avenue, Morristown
07960; (973) 267–3465

BOONTON HISTORIC DISTRICT
Boonton

BULL'S ISLAND RECREATION AREA
2185 Daniel Bray Highway,
(Route 29), Stockton 08559;
(609) 397–2949

COOPER MILL
Route 24, Chester 07930;
(908) 879–5463

CROSS ESTATE GARDENS
Old Jockey Hollow Road,
Bernardsville 07924;
(973) 539–2016

DUKE FARM AND GARDENS
Somerville 08876;
(908) 722–3700

HUNTERDON HISTORICAL MUSEUM
56 Main Street, Clinton 08809;
(908) 735–4101

MILLBROOK VILLAGE
Old Mine Road, Millbrook;
(908) 841–9531 or 841–9520

VAN CAMPEN INN
Old Mine Road, Walpack Center
07881; (973) 729–7392

WHIPPANY RAILWAY MUSEUM
1 Railroad Plaza, Route 10,
Whippany 07981;
(973) 887–8177

WORLD APOSTOLATE OF FATIMA AND THE IMMACULATE HEART OF MARY SHRINE
Mountain View Road,
Washington 07882;
(908) 689–1700

Selected Regional Information Centers, Chambers of Commerce, and Visitor Centers in Northern New Jersey and the Upper Delaware Valley

Skylands Regional Tourism Council,
3117 Route 10E, Denville 07834,
(800) 4–SKYLAN

Somerset County Chamber of Commerce,
64 West End Avenue, Somerville 08876,
(908) 725–1552;
Web site: http://www.somerset-countychamber.org

Central New Jersey

The central swath of New Jersey constitutes the narrowest portion of this wasp-waisted state. From the mouth of the Raritan River at South Amboy to the Delaware River at Trenton is barely 35 miles—no wonder this is the crossroads of New Jersey, the place chosen for early New York-to-Philadelphia transportation enterprises such as the Delaware and Raritan Canal and the Camden and Amboy Railroad of the 1830s. More than fifty years before these technological marvels were undertaken, George Washington led his troops westward across Central Jersey in a successful attempt to escape the British threat in New York. Crossing the Delaware near Trenton (a state park commemorates the event today), he struck back at the British and Hessians in one of history's great surprise attacks. In our own day the central corridor of New Jersey is where the famous New Jersey Turnpike makes its dash from the northeastern to the southwestern part of the state.

Central New Jersey, however, is not just a place of comings and goings. Here, at Trenton, is the state capital; here, too, are two of America's finest universities, Rutgers (in New Brunswick) and Princeton. Old industries, like china and glass, and new ones, like electronics and refining, have found Central Jersey a place conducive to growth.

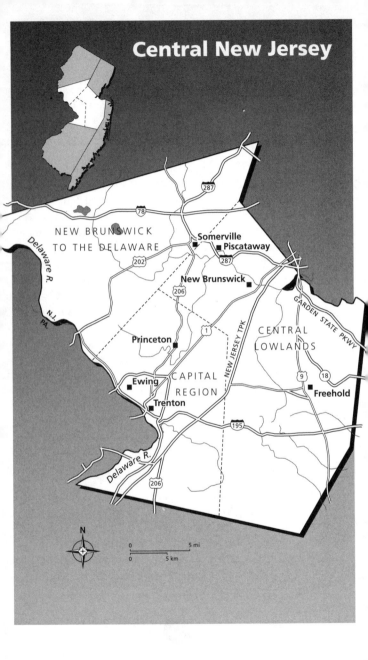

Central New Jersey

NEW BRUNSWICK
TO THE DELAWARE

Somerville

Piscataway

New Brunswick

Princeton

CENTRAL
LOWLANDS

Ewing

CAPITAL
REGION

Trenton

Freehold

Delaware R.

N.J.

PA.

Delaware R.

GARDEN STATE PKWY

NEW JERSEY TPK

N

0   5 mi

0   5 km

CENTRAL NEW JERSEY'S TOP PICKS

Museum of Early Trades and Crafts

Great Swamp

Golf House

Hunterdon Historical Museum

Hunterdon House

Flemington Cut Glass Company

Black River and Western Railroad

The Stockton Inn

Delaware and Raritan Canal State Park

Lambertville

Howell Living History Farm

Drumthwacket

The Art Museum, Princeton University

Forrestal at Princeton

Old Barracks Museum

"Little Italy"

New Jersey Vietnam Veterans' Memorial

Kuser Farm Mansion

Bordentown

Bellevue

Naval Air Warfare Center at Lakehurst

Historic Allaire Village

Biplane Adventure Tours Ltd.

Zimmerli Art Museum

Hutcheson Memorial Forest

All such boundaries are imprecise, but we might say that central New Jersey begins where the state's northern uplands give way to the gently rolling hills of Somerset County horse country, and it extends south almost to the edges of the Pine Barrens. The western border is, of course, the Delaware River. On the east is the coastal plain, but because the Jersey Shore has such a distinct character of its own, we'll save it for a later chapter.

Note: The orientation in this chapter is east to west, from New Brunswick to the Delaware River; then south, through the Capital Region; and, finally, counter-clockwise as we move back north to the Raritan Valley of the Central Lowlands.

New Brunswick to the Delaware

When *Mead Hall* at *Drew University* was damaged by fire in August 1989, the administration determined to salvage some good from the disaster. They decided to restore the 1830s Gibbons family mansion with as much historic precision as possible. The building is now a period piece: The wallpaper and flooring duplicate the originals, and a number of original marble fireplaces were uncovered in the restoration.

Mead Hall at Drew University, Madison 07940, (973) 408–3000, houses the president's and executive offices and is used for meetings and student seminars. It is open Monday through Friday 9:00 A.M.–5:00 P.M., except during holidays and long holiday weekends. There is no admission charge.

AUTHORS' FAVORITE ATTRACTIONS IN CENTRAL NEW JERSEY

Art Museum, Princeton University
Delaware Water Gap National Recreation Area
Hunterdon County Courthouse
New Jersey State Police Museum and Learning Center
New Jersey Vietnam Veterans' Memorial
Northlandz
Old Barracks Museum

TOP ANNUAL EVENTS IN CENTRAL NEW JERSEY

Note: Schedules may vary; call ahead.

New Jersey Flower and Garden Show, *Somerset; February;*
(732) 919-7660

Shad Festival, *Lambertville; April; (609) 397-0055*

Tour of Somerville; *May; (908) 725-0461*

Heritage Days, *Trenton; June; (609) 695-7107*

Annual Battle of Monmouth, *Manalapan; June; (732) 462-6855*

The Magic of Alexandria Up, Up Away Balloon Festival,
Pittstown; August; (908) 735-0870

George Washington Crossing the Delaware,
Washington Crossing State Park, Titusville; December 25;
(609) 737-0623

Fortunately not all the physical remains of earlier times had to be restored from ashes. Many of the everyday objects associated with life in the seventeenth and eighteenth centuries simply collected dust in attics, cellars, and barns, and if they stayed out of the way of zealous spring cleaners, they survived into our own age to be treasured as antiques. The preservation of these artifacts, particularly those associated with the world of work, is the mission of the *Museum of Early Trades and Crafts* in Madison.

The heart of the museum's holdings is the Edgar Law Land collection of eighteenth- and nineteenth-century tools and products that pertain to New Jersey homes, farms, trades, and shop crafts. The museum interprets a time when most New Jerseyans lived on farms or in country villages. The collection encompasses both common and unique everyday products of the home, from horn spoons to bobbin-lace pillows, as well as the tools of carpenters, coopers, tinsmiths, masons, cobblers, wheelwrights, bookbinders, and stonecutters plus unusual lens-making tools and early medical equipment.

Exhibits, many of which feature hands-on discovery areas, include a recreated colonial kitchen, shoemaker's shop, one-room schoolhouse, and changing exhibits. The museum also offers educational programs for people of all ages, including school programs, adult tours, and special programs every Saturday throughout the school year.

The museum, a nonprofit organization founded in 1970, is housed in the former James Library building, which was built in 1900. The building is listed on the National Register of Historic Places as an excellent example of the Richardson Romanesque style. It features stained-glass windows, stenciling, a glass-floor gallery, and an 1899 Seth Thomas tower clock.

The Museum of Early Trades and Crafts, Main Street and Green Village Road, Madison 07940, (973)

377–2982, is open year-round. Call for hours and admission fees.

There is one part of New Jersey, just 26 miles west of Times Square, that has changed very little, if at all, since the days when coopers made barrels and wheelwrights wrought wheels. The **Great Swamp** has, in fact, changed hardly at all over the past few thousand years. It isn't going to change during the foreseeable future, either, because this more-than-7,400-acre tract of wetland and forest is protected as a national wildlife refuge.

A New Jersey Lord

The comfortable residential suburb of Stirling, which lies just south of the Great Swamp National Wildlife Refuge, is named after an American-born aristocrat named William Alexander. An American aristocrat? Yes—and not just in the figurative sense of wealth and power, which Alexander also enjoyed. Born in New York, and owner of a magnificent estate in Basking Ridge, New Jersey, Alexander was a direct descendant of the Scottish earls of Stirling.

Despite his noble rank, Lord Stirling was an active and effective participant on the American side in the Revolution. He commanded New Jersey's first body of Continental troops and was soon elevated to the rank of general. He executed a daring strategic retreat at the Battle of Long Island, captured a British supply ship off Sandy Hook, and brilliantly commanded American artillery at the Battle of Monmouth. With Stirling's untimely death at Albany before the war's end, George Washington lost a good friend and a valuable commander—a man whom, oddly enough given what Washington was fighting for, he always called "my Lord."

The stories of how the swamp came to be and how it came to be saved are equally interesting. At one time the land occupied by the swamp—and a good deal more of what was to become north-central New Jersey—was covered by a 200-foot-deep lake, fed by meltwater from the receding Wisconsin Ice Sheet of 10,000 years ago. This vast inland sea, called Lake Passaic by modern geologists, did not drain off until the retreating ice had uncovered a gap at Little Falls, through which water could pour downstream to the Atlantic, but the bottom of Lake Passaic never dried out completely. Its understructure of dense clay was a poor absorber of water, and wetlands were created along a long swath of North Jersey, extending from the Great Swamp to Fairfield's Great Piece Meadow. Three centuries of white settlement around the fringes of the swamp failed to result in any permanent penetration of its deepest recesses. In the 1950s it was still left to wood ducks and bitterns, to fox, otter, and muskrat.

In 1959, however, the death knell of the swamp was very nearly sounded, in the form of a report from the Port Authority of New York and New Jersey that favored the vast wetland as the site for a proposed jetport. Projects like this had traditionally been viewed as the triumph of civilization over "wasteland," but this time a substantial portion of the citizenry of the surrounding towns did not agree. They banded together to form the Great Swamp Committee and set about raising the necessary funds to buy the threatened land and present it to the U.S. Department of Interior for use as a refuge. The initial 3,000-acre tract was so dedicated in 1964, and the property in federal hands has since more than doubled. Eighty percent of the swamp is now protected, more than 3,600 acres of it as wilderness, free from motorized traffic and permanent construction.

The **_Great Swamp Outdoor Education Center_** in Chatham is an excellent place to begin your visit. The center, open daily from 9:00 A.M. to 4:30 P.M. (closed July and August), provides an introduction to the geology and ecology of the area. A handicapped-accessible boardwalk trail and an observation blind are here as well. The center is at 247 Southern Boulevard, Chatham 07928, (973) 635–6629.

A wildlife observation center, with observation blinds, trails, and rest rooms that are handicapped-accessible, borders the management and wilderness sectors of the property. A system of $8^1/_2$ miles of marked trails extends through the wilderness. Maps are available at the headquarters, as are checklists of the bird, reptile, amphibian, and mammal species, as well as common wildflowers that have been documented here.

The Great Swamp National Wildlife Refuge headquarters is located at 152 Pleasant Plains Road (exit 30A off I–287), Basking Ridge 07920, (973) 425–1222 and is open daily throughout the year. The south gate of the refuge, on Pleasant Plains Road, is closed between dusk and 8:00 A.M.; the north gate is always closed.

A far cry from the Great Swamp's primeval disorder are the manicured lawns of **_Golf House,_** the United States Golf Association's museum and library in Far Hills. Golf House, a magnificent Georgian Colonial mansion built in 1919, houses the most complete collection of golf memorabilia, artwork, and equipment extant in the United States.

At the Golf House in Far Hills, the United States Golf Association (USGA) exhibits the sport's rich heritage.

Visitors to Golf House can take a systematic, educational approach to the USGA's interpretive exhibits or simply drop in to see a splendid assortment of golfing curiosities and association items. The history of the game is traced from its earliest Scottish beginnings and is chronicled by examples of the balls and clubs used during different eras as well as by explanations of the evolution of rules and course maintenance. Videos of golfing greats even make it possible to compare swings.

Treasured artifacts of the sport on display at Golf House include the historic collapsible six iron used by astronaut Alan Shepard to drive a ball on the moon in 1971, an entire roomful of Robert T. Jones, Jr., memorabilia, and the largest public golf library in the world—over 13,000 volumes.

Golf House Museum and Library, Liberty Corner Road, Far Hills 07931, (908) 234–2300, is open weekdays 9:00 A.M.–5:00 P.M., and weekends 10:00 A.M.–4:00 P.M. Admission is free.

One of the premier rock gardens in the East has been "growing" since it was first conceived in the late 1930s. The **Leonard J. Buck Garden**, nestled in a thirty-three-acre wooded stream valley, is actually a series of alpine and woodland gardens.

Tucked among rock outcroppings are a bewildering variety of rare and exotic rock garden plants, all placed so as to appear as if they were occurring naturally. Leafy trails connecting the outcroppings are lined with wildflowers. A profusion of heaths and heathers, all varieties of *Calluna* and *Erica*, flourish in a raised peninsula bed at the entrance to the Visitors' Center.

On a slope behind the center is the F. Gordon Foster Hardy Fern Collection, which includes Christmas, northern maidenhair, and rare fern species such as the tiny rusty woodsia, and painted and autumn ferns from Japan.

Although Buck Garden's peak bloom period occurs in spring, there are splashes of color—or at least a welcome green—almost every week of the year. The garden is maintained by the Somerset County Park

Commission, which also oversees the Colonial Park Arboretum and its magnificent Rudolf W. van der Goot Rose Garden, with more than 3,000 roses of more than 200 varieties.

The Leonard J. Buck Garden, 11 Layton Road, Far Hills 07931, is open Monday through Friday 10:00 A.M.–4:00 P.M. Saturday 10: 00 A.M.–5:00 P.M., Sunday noon–5:00 P.M., and closed on weekends and major holidays in December, January, and February. A $1.00 per person donation is requested. For information on the garden and/or the arboretum, call the park commission at (908) 234–2677.

It's rumored that when chefs want a night out, they head to **Ryland Inn** for regional French cuisine prepared by owner-chef Craig Shelton. The restaurant, in a restored late-eighteenth-century home, features creations such as sauteed soft-shell crabs with vegetables *a la grecque* and roasted baby lamb with oven-dried tomatoes, artichokes, and basil. It's on Route 22W in Whitehouse, (908) 534–4011, and serves lunch Monday through Friday and dinner nightly. Jackets are required.

Long ago the Delaware River met up with the ancient Kittatinny Mountains, which, once eroded practically to the level of the river's crest, were in the process of rising once again. Rather than go around, the river held its course, sawing downward through the rocks. The result is the **Delaware Water Gap National Recreation Area,** with the largest and highest cliffs in the state.

If you want to scale the cliffs, **Mountain Sports, Inc.,** in Clinton operates Mountain Sports Adventure School, the only rock -and ice-climbing school in New Jersey that has been accredited by the American Mountain Guides Association. The school offers numerous courses in rock- and ice-climbing, rents equipment, and can provide the permits required to rock-climb in state parks.

Mountain Sports, Inc., 1802 Highway 31 Suite 2, Clinton 08809, (908) 638–5700, is open Monday and Wednesday through Friday 10:00 A.M.–7:00 P.M., Saturday 10:00 A.M.–5:00 P.M., and Sunday 10:00 A.M.–4:00 P.M. Closed Tuesday and holidays.

Like Waterloo Village, Fosterfields, and the Museum of Early Trades and Crafts, **_Hunterdon Historical Museum_** provides a glimpse into a domestic past that was, historically, just the day before yesterday but seems, in technological terms, as remote as the Middle Ages. Located on the South Branch of the Raritan River just north of I–78, the museum centers on what was formerly the most important building in these parts: the Old Red Mill, in which waterpower at one time ground grain, flaxseed, limestone, graphite, and talc. Today the mill exhibits suggest the rural life of the nineteenth- through early-twentieth-century periods in the Delaware Valley. In many ways things didn't change that much on the farms and in backcountry villages through that long stretch of time.

The "village" that clusters near the Old Red Mill is a string of period structures, tucked neatly between the river and the 150-foot limestone cliffs that provided much of the mill's work. Here are an old general store/post office, a one-room schoolhouse, a log cabin, a blacksmith shop, and wagon sheds. Unique to this museum are the remains of Mulligan's lime quarry, including office, dynamite shed, lime kilns, and stone crusher.

If you are in the Clinton area between mid-June and the end of August, look into the museum's Concerns in the Park program. Each week the natural outdoor amphitheater, created by the cliffs near the mill, is the site for jazz, folk, ethnic, or old-time music.

Hunterdon Historical Museum, 56 Main Street, Clinton 08809, (908) 735–4101, is open April 1 through October 31, Tuesday through Saturday 10:00 A.M.–4:00 P.M.; Sunday noon–5:00 P.M. (last admission tickets are sold one hour before closing). Admission is $3.00 for adults, $2.00 for senior citizens, and $1.00 for children ages six through sixteen.

The *Hunterdon Art Center*, housed in a nineteenth-century stone gristmill, which is on the National Register of Historic Places, is Hunterdon County's visual arts center. Galleries feature works by local and internationally renowned artists. The Anne Steel Marsh collection includes more than 350 contemporary prints by artists such as Ben Shahn, Salvador Dali, and Edward Coker. The sales gallery features handcrafted items by regional artists. The center is at 7 Lower Center Street, Clinton 08809, (908) 735–8415. Exhibits are open Wednesday through Sunday 11:00 A.M.–5:00 P.M. The sales gallery is open Tuesday through Sunday 10:00 A.M.–5:00 P.M.

The Victorian *Leigh Way Bed & Breakfast* provides clean, air-conditioned bedrooms, private baths, and a central location at 66 Leigh Street, Clinton 08809, (908) 735–4311.

The *Vollendam Wind Mill and Museum,* an operational, wind-driven gristmill that is a replica of a Dutch windmill, stands 60 feet high and has 68-foot-long sail arms. The museum, at 231 Adamic Hill Road, Milford 08848, (908) 995–4365, is open Saturdays and Sundays noon–4:30 P.M. in spring and summer. Admission is $2.50 for adults, $1.00 for children.

The Ship Inn, an authentic British pub, has fourteen British draft ales and hard cider on tap, as well as a great selection of single-malt whiskies. The cuisine is from England, Ireland, Scotland, and Wales. The inn, at 61 Bridge Street, Milford 08848, (908) 995–7007, is open daily for lunch from 11:30 A.M.; Monday through Thursday and on Sunday for dinner 4:00–9:00 P.M.; and Friday and Saturday for dinner 4:00–10:00 P.M.

From time to time on back-road rambles, we pass by a house that looks so interesting from the outside we're tempted to knock on the door and ask for a tour. ***Hunterdon House,*** a huge, Italianate-style mansion, is

A Martian Invasion

*T*he *small towns of New Jersey have been invaded by strip malls, suburban developers, and multinational corporations trying to escape Manhattan real estate prices. But as far as we know, only one Jersey town has ever been invaded by Martians.*

When Orson Welles broadcast his notoriously realistic radio adaptation of H.G. Wells' The War of the Worlds *on October 30, 1938, he had the Martians' capsules land in Grover's Mill, a hamlet just a few miles from Princeton Junction. Grover's Mill was rural enough for the invaders to launch their attack in relative obscurity, yet convenient for their march on New York and Philadelphia. What more could any ambitious commuter desire?*

such a place. Fortunately it's also a B&B, so visitors are welcome to tour anytime and stay overnight if there's a room available. This recently renovated 1864 mansion has seven guest rooms. The owners tell us that the Daisy Apgar Suite, with its wicker-appointed sitting room and its bedroom with an antique carved rosewood double bed, is a favorite with honeymooners, as is the William Apgar Room, with a working fireplace and Eastlake-carved cathedral-style queen bed. The house is at 12 Bridge Street, Frenchtown 08825, (908) 996–3632.

Local produce and products—including hand-picked wild mushrooms—are staples at the **Frenchtown Inn,** which also does its own smoking and sausage making. The restaurant, in an 1805 restored building that was formerly a hotel, consistently wins three- and four-star ratings from dining guides. Menu offerings include Atlantic salmon, roast rack of lamb, and duck. The restaurant is at 7 Bridge Street, Frenchtown, (908) 996–3300. It's open for lunch Tuesday through Saturday noon–2:00 P.M.; for dinner Tuesday through Friday 6:00–9:00 P.M., Saturday 5:30–9:30 P.M., and Sunday 5:30–8:30 P.M.; for Sunday brunch, noon–2:45 P.M. A prix-fixe dinner is available Saturday for $45.

Before you leave Frenchtown, stop at **French Country Pottery,** 52 Bridge Street, which sells hand-sculpted pottery by Sandy McKenzie Schmidt. Nearby, the **Blackburn and Yates Gallery** features works by local contemporary artists as well as handmade jewelry and Japanese *raku* pottery.

The town of Flemington, with its many factory-outlet stores, has become a haven for shoppers. One of the most popular continues to be **Flemington Cut Glass**

Company, the oldest maker of hand-cut crystal and glass in the country. For more than seventy-five years, this Delaware Valley firm has developed its own patterns and done hand cutting and polishing of glassware on its Flemington premises. As interesting as the glass-cutting operation is to watch, it's a fair bet that most visitors to Flemington come to purchase glassware in display rooms, advertised by the firm as holding the largest selection in the world. In addition to its own merchandise, Flemington sells first-quality products, seconds, and closeouts by manufacturers such as Riedel and Schott-Zwiesel. Flemington Glass Company, 156 Main Street, Flemington 08822, (908) 782–3017, is open Monday through Saturday 10:00 A.M.–5:30 P.M. and Sunday 11:00 A.M.–5:30 P.M. All you need for admission is a burning urge to shop.

In 1935 the eyes of the world were on the town of Flemington when Bruno Richard Hauptmann, accused of kidnapping and killing the baby of Charles and Anne Morrow Lindbergh, was put on trial in the *Hunterdon County Courthouse* at the corner of Main and Court Streets. Reporters stayed across the street at the Union Hotel (now a restaurant). At the end of the "Trial of the Century," which lasted six weeks, Hauptmann was found guilty and was executed on April 3, 1936, at Trenton State Prison. Each summer, over five weekends, semiprofessional actors re-create the trial in the courthouse, using dialogue taken directly from the transcripts. Call (908) 782–2610 for dates and/or reservations.

The ever-civilized British have made the act of drinking tea practically an art form. We expect that after hours of wandering through Flemington's shops, a stop at

Canterbury Corner, "A Real English Tea Shop," will give you an appreciation of just how bracing a "cuppa" can be. Service, naturally, begins with "elevenses" and home-baked scones; continues with lunch; and concludes with afternoon tea, served from 3:00–5:00 P.M. daily. The tea shop is at the corner of Church Street and Central Avenue, (908) 788–5547.

At *Northlandz,* one of the state's newest attractions, the Great American Railway—the world's largest miniature railway—has 125 trains that scoot along 8 miles of track through a miniaturized landscape of 35-foot mountains, 40-foot bridges, and handcrafted cities and villages. At one point a triple-spiral, triple-track trestle bridge provides a route for three trains through desert canyons. Also here is a ninety-four-room mansion at the Doll Museum, complete with indoor swimming pool and ballroom; it exhibits more than 150 dolls from around the world. In the American Music Hall there is a magnificent 2,000-pipe organ rocks the walls of the 250-seat theater several times a day.

The sixteen-acre attraction is the culmination of a twenty-five-year project by Bruce Williams Zaccagnino. It's at 495 Highway 202 in Flemington 08820, (908) 782–4022, and open daily 10:00 A.M. to 6:00 P.M., Fridays until 8:00 P.M. Admission is $12.75 for adults, $8.75 for children ages three through twelve, free under three.

An enduring American icon is the steam locomotive. It's been more than forty years since diesels began to outnumber steamers on the nation's railroads, and three decades have passed since the iron horse became extinct in regular United States commercial operation. Still, we can't let go of steam. A recently published guide to rail museums and tourist railroads listed nearly ninety operations that run regularly scheduled or special steam-powered trains. Two of them are right here in New Jersey—one in Allaire State Park (which we'll get to later) and another headquartered in the small central-western New Jersey town of Ringoes. This is the **Black River and Western Railroad,** which offers a one-hour ride between Ringoes and Flemington along a former branch of the Pennsylvania Railroad.

On Saturdays, Sundays, and holidays from mid-April through November, the BR&WRR operates a 1937 Alco 2-8-0, hauling a consist (complement) of former Jersey Central and Lackawanna coaches and two open observation cars. What's a 2-8-0? The first number refers to the nonpowered pilot wheels, the second to the coupled drive wheels, and the third to the trailing wheels beneath the cab. Thus, a 2-8-0 has two pilot wheels, four coupled axles with eight drivers, and no trailing wheels.

If the means of motive power isn't all that important and you simply want to enjoy the ride through the rolling West Jersey farm country, you can board the BR&WRR's ex-Pennsylvania diesel-electric motor car Number 4666 at either Ringoes or Flemington on weekdays (except Mondays) during July and August.

For the latest schedule and fare information, contact the Black River and Western Railroad, P.O. Box 200, Ringoes 08551, (908) 782–9600. The BR&WRR's restored 1854 station and snack bar is on Route 579, near the intersection of routes 202 and 31.

In 1933 lyricist Lorenz Hart and composer Richard Rodgers visited **The Stockton Inn.** Inspired by the inn and its environs, they wrote "There's a Small Hotel with a

Wishing Well." Rodgers and Hart weren't the only artists inspired by the inn, built as a private residence in 1710. Kurt Wiese, illustrator of the original book *Bambi,* painted murals on the dining-room walls. Bandleader Paul Whiteman kept a regular table at the inn, which came to be known as "Colligan's" for the Colligan family who owned it, and signed off his radio and TV shows by announcing he was going to dinner at "Ma Colligan's." A table favored by Dorothy Parker, Robert Benchley, S. J. Perelman, and friends became known as The Algonquin Roundtable, in honor of their New York City meeting place.

The "Small Hotel with a Wishing Well" is still a popular meeting spot for lunch and dinner. Cuisine is contemporary American, and meals are served in the dining room or in The Garden—complete with waterfalls and trout pond. Prices are moderate (dinner entrées generally run under $20), but the best deal in town may well be the three-course Early Dinner for $11.95, served 4:30–6:30 P.M. Monday through Friday, except holidays.

Overnight guests can choose from a variety of accommodations, including a suite, with gas fireplace, in the main Inn; a loft, with fireplace, in the 1832 Wagon House; or a suite, with a queen-size canopy bed and fireplace, in the 1850 Federal House.

The Stockton Inn, One Main Street, Route 29, Stockton 08559, (609) 397–1250, is open for lunch Monday through Saturday, dinners nightly, and Sunday brunch.

Built in the late 1700s, the elegant ***Woolverton Inn***, just a mile from the Delaware Canal and River, stands graciously amidst ten acres of century-old oak and apple trees. Eight of the inn's ten rooms are in the three-story stone manor house; the others are in a converted 1800s carriage house. All have private baths and air conditioning; two have working fireplaces, and two have Jacuzzi tubs. The lovely veranda is a wonderful place to rock away idle hours; the elegantly appointed, fireplaced living room, a charming spot for tea on a cold winter day. The innkeepers serve a full country breakfast and will provide lunch and/or dinner on request.

The Woolverton Inn is at 6 Woolverton Road, Stockton 08559, 1–888–AN INN 4U or (609) 397–0802. Room rates, which include breakfast, range from $80 to $140 on weekdays and from $105 to $190 on weekends. There is a two-night minimum stay on weekends and a three-night minimum stay on holiday weekends.

You have to go a long way in New Jersey to drive through a covered bridge—to Sergeantsville, in fact. The *Green Sergeants Bridge* on Route 604 is the last, and only, covered bridge on a public road in the state. Built in 1872, it was scheduled to be demolished in the 1950s, but a group of citizens banded together and saved it. The 73-foot-8-inch wooden bridge over the Wickecheoke Creek is on its original abutments. For more information call (609) 397–3240.

Before the great days of railroad, canals were king. A century and a half ago, when the first toylike locomotives were begining to chuff and sputter along weak and uneven track, it was considered a tremendous advantage to be able to ship freight along the slow, smooth canals, rather than over the treacherous carriage roads of the day—thus the enthusiasm with which New Jerseyans greeted the opening of the Delaware and Raritan Canal in 1834.

From the day it opened, the Delaware and Raritan Canal was one of America's busiest waterways. Along its 44-mile length between Trenton and New Brunswick, coal traveled east from Pennsylvania to New York, finished goods were sent west from the great metropolis, and New Jersey produce was shipped beyond the valleys where it was grown to help boost the agricultural fame of the "garden" state. The canal became so much a part of the fabric of life in New Jersey that even though it last showed a profit in 1892, it remained open to traffic for another forty years before finally succumbing to the highways and railroads.

A 44-mile canal makes a mighty big white elephant. After the D&R was closed to barge traffic, it was used to channel water for farm irrigation and for industrial and residential use. During this period the canal began to attract recreational users; the old towpaths, along which draft animals at one time pulled the barges, made ideal hiking trails, and fishing and boating were easy along such a long, calm stretch of water, with only fourteen locks between Trenton and New Brunswick. Eventually the state legislature responded to what had been a *de facto* recreational use pattern and created the **Delaware and Raritan Canal State Park.**

The D&R State Park is probably the only such entity in America that is 60 miles long and, for most of that length, only 25 yards across. In addition to those portions of the route that were never filled in (sections near Bordentown and New Brunswick), the park includes the 22-mile

The Delaware and Raritan Canal, opened in 1834, has been a popular waterway for both business and pleasure.

feeder channel that extends along the east bank of the Delaware from Bulls Island to Trenton.

There are two major developed centers for visitors in the D&R State Park: near Blackwells Mills, off Route 27 southeast of New Brunswick; and at Bulls Island, on the Delaware north of Lambertville. The Blackwells Mills site is the location of the main park office and information center, whereas Bulls Island has seventy campsites open April 1 to November 1, half of which may be reserved. (Contact Bull's Island Recreation Area, 2185 Daniel Bray Highway, Stockton 08559, (609–397–2949). Small boats are welcome throughout the park, as long as no gasoline engines are involved. Information on privately operated canoe-rental services is available at park headquarters or by mail. Park headquarters can also supply details on the approximately fifty park access points, about half of which offer parking.

Delaware and Raritan Canal State Park (mailing address: 625 Canal Road, Somerset 08873; 732–873–3050) is open throughout the year. Contact the park super-intendent at the above address regarding camping season and regulations.

There are big doings in *Lambertville* during the last full weekend in April. Each year the town hosts the Shad Festival—a nationally recognized event that features artists, crafters, and the environment. Through shad-hauling and fish-tagging demonstrations, the festival helps focus on the importance of keeping the Delaware River clean. The aroma of cooked shad permeates the town as street vendors serve it up barbecued and fried, and down by the river the Boat Club and Chamber of Commerce host grilled shad dinners.

To watch an artist at work, visit the *Bernard Unger-leider Art Studio* between 11:00 A.M. and 5:00 P.M. Saturdays and Sundays. Mr. Ungerleider, working in oils and pastels, paints and exhibits his portraits, landscapes, and still lifes in his studio loft at 23 Bridge Street, Lambertville 08530. If you want to visit during the week, call him for an appointment at (609) 397–2239. *The Sojourner,* at 26 Bridge Street, (609) 397–8849, sells clothing from Indonesia, Japan, Ecuador, Peru, and Guatemala and stocks a large assortment of loose beads as well as contemporary and ethnic jewelry.

De Anna's, at 18 South Main Street in Lambertville, specializes in homemade pastas and sauces. The restaurant has no liquor license, does not allow smoking, and does not accept credit cards. It does, however, have delicious food. It's open for lunch, Tuesday through Friday, and for dinner, Wednesday through Sunday. Reservations are a must on weekends; call (609) 397–8957.

If you're looking for a bit more ambience (or a predinner cocktail), *Lambertville Station* serves American cuisine in the town's restored Victorian train station. Specialties include shrimp almondine, pan-blackened swordfish, and fine aged beef; and from January to March, the chefs serve up special wild-game dishes. The restaurant is on Bridge Street at the Delaware River, Lambertville, (609) 397–8300. Lunch is served Monday through Saturday; dinner nightly; and brunch every Sunday.

A California Connection

*P*icturesque little Lambertville, with its upscale bistros, inns, and galleries, has been linked with New Hope, Pennsylvania, ever since Samuel Coryell began running his ferry across the Delaware River in 1732. More than a century later, the little town made a connection with history across a much greater distance. James Marshall, a descendant of Declaration of Independence signer John Hart, was born in Lambertville and lived in the Marshall family's brick house, which still stands at 60 Bridge Street. While supervising the building of Sutter's mill in northern California in 1848, Marshall discovered the nuggets that set off the fabled Gold Rush of the following year.

Marshall, by the way, died broke.

Next door, each of the forty-five rooms at **The Inn at Lambertville Station** is uniquely decorated with antiques from throughout the world. It's a perfect spot for those who like the charm of a B&B but the amenities of a small luxury hotel. The inn is at 11 Bridge Street, Lambertville 08530; call (609) 397–8300 or, from out of state, (800) 524–1091.

The **Lambertville House Historic Inn,** built in 1812, was once a stagecoach stop serving U.S. presidents and dignitaries traveling between Philadelphia and New York. Today the beautifully restored inn, with its imposing facade of quarried stone etched with wrought-iron balustrades, welcomes guests looking for gracious accommodations. The twenty-five large, elegantly appointed rooms and suites are furnished with antiques and period reproductions, and most have their own fireplace and jetted tub. Many have balconies overlooking the courtyard or town. The inn is at 32 Bridge Street, Lambertville 08530, (609) 397–0200 or (888) 867–8859. Rates for a standard double range from $155 to $199.

Capital Region

The 130-acre **Howell Living History Farm** has been a working farm for 200 years and is being restored to operate like a typical New Jersey family farm circa 1900. Special programs throughout the year are planned around the actual seasonal activities of a working farm. A self-guided tour for visitors includes thirty points of interest, including a sheep barn, a chicken house, a wagon house, and an icehouse. There's even a genuine outhouse! Special hands-on programs for groups are offered throughout the year.

Howell Living History Farm, 101 Hunter Road, Titusville 08560, (609) 737–3299, is open daily except Mondays and holidays. Call for specific hours. Admission is free.

The town of Princeton is forever secondary in the public mind to the great institution that it harbors— Princeton University, New Jersey's entry in the Ivy League—but there is more to Princeton than its university, as a ride down Stockton Street (Route 206) will show. Here are two magnificent mansions, both currently being restored and both at one time or another having been the official residence of the governors of New Jersey.

Morven, the older of the two mansions, was, for more than 200 years, the home of the Stockton family. Richard Stockton, signer of the Declaration of Independence, built his original house here in 1701 on land he purchased from Philadelphia's founder, William Penn. The present structure is an agglomeration of additions to that early home, most of them added in the mid-eighteenth century, when the Georgian style predominated. The mansion, located on Stockton Street at Liberty Place, is open to visitors on Wednesdays. Admission is free. For more information call (609) 683–1514.

The present executive mansion is *Drumthwacket,* a mile past Morven on Stockton Street. Drumthwacket is a stately Greek Revival structure, with six great central pillars, looking for all the world like an antebellum Southern mansion transported to the Delaware Valley.

Drumthwacket was built in 1835 by Charles Olden, who later became governor of New Jersey. His building was the original central, columned portion; the wings were added by a later owner in the 1890s. Drumthwacket is open to the public on Wednesdays between noon and 2:00 P.M. Admission is free. For information call (609) 683–0057.

The permanent collection of *The Art Museum, Princeton University,* ranges from ancient to contemporary art and concentrates geographically on the Mediterranean regions, Western Europe, China, the United States, and Latin America. There is an outstanding collection of Greek and Roman antiquities, including Roman mosaics from Princeton University's excavations in Antioch. The collection of Western European paintings includes outstanding examples from the early Renaissance through the nineteenth century. Among the greatest strengths are Chinese art, with significant holdings in bronzes, tomb figures, and paintings; and pre-Columbian art, with remarkable examples of the art of the Maya. The museum has important collections of old-master prints and a comprehensive collection of original photographs. Princeton University's John B. Putnam, Jr., Memorial Collection of twentieth-century sculpture, located throughout the campus, includes works by such modern masters as Henry Moore, Alexander Calder, Pablo Picasso, and Jacques Lipchitz.

The Art Museum, Princeton University, near Nassau Hall and Firestone Library, Nassau Street, Princeton 08544, (609) 452–3787, is open Tuesday through Saturday 10:00 A.M.–4:45 P.M., and Sunday 1:00–4:45

An ancient Chinese sculpture circa 1250 A.D.
can be found at Princeton's art museum.

P.M. The museum is closed on major holidays.
Admission is free.

Champagne and live piano music set the mood for an
elegant Sunday brunch, served from 11:00 A.M.–2:30
P.M., at *Forrestal at Princeton.* Breakfast specialties,

poached salmon, shrimp, pâtés, and salads are served at the gleaming brass buffet tables, and chefs are on hand to prepare omelets and slice beef. Save room for the dessert buffet and complimentary glass of champagne. The cost is $23.95 for adults; half price for children ages three to twelve; free for children under three. On holidays the cost increases, depending on what is being served. If seafood is more to your liking, stop by the inn's Homestate Cafe Restaurant Saturday evening for the Beyond the Sea buffet, featuring grilled lobster, peel-and-eat shrimp, caviar, and homemade salads and breads (filet mignon is also available).

Forrestal at Princeton is at 100 College Road East, Princeton 08544, (609) 452–7800. Complimentary valet parking is available, and reservations are recommended.

Behind Palmer Square, near the Public Library, is **Princeton Cemetery,** final resting place of politicians and presidents including Aaron Burr, Grover Cleveland, and Jonathan Edwards. Pick up a map at the super-intendent's house near the entrance. The cemetery, 29 Greenview Avenue, is always open. For information call (609) 924–1369.

Stop in at the **Nassau Inn**'s Yankee Doodle Tap Room for a drink, a bite, or just to see Norman Rockwell's 13-foot-long mural, *Yankee Doodle Dandy*. The inn, which has been accommodating weary travelers since 1756, is at 10 Palmer Square, Princeton 08542, (609) 921–7500.

Trenton, the capital of New Jersey, was in 1776 a tiny village of no more than one hundred houses, important chiefly as the head of navigation on the Delaware River. Since Christmas of that year, however, it has loomed inestimably larger in American history, because of George Washington's crossing of the ice-clogged Delaware and defeat of Great Britain's Hessian mercenaries in the Battle of Trenton.

Tradition holds that at the time of the battle, Hessians were quartered in an eighteen-year-old stone building located near the spot where the New Jersey State House stands today. After having survived many uses and a few dates with the wrecker's ball, this venerable structure survives today as the ***Old Barracks Museum.***

A Depression-Era Experiment

*L*ocated about 20 miles east of Trenton, the town of Roosevelt was founded in 1935 as a community called Jersey Homesteads. Incorporating a women's clothing factory and a 40-acre farm, the settlement would provide a new home for garment workers previously confined to the tenements of New York and Philadelphia. Launched with both government and private funds, the community was to be an experiment in cooperative ownership of factory, farm, and stores, with an equal distribution of profits. New housing was built, and attractive mortgage terms offered.

The Homesteads' manufacturing and agricultural ventures met with little success; within a few years the community was opened to everyone and the cooperative scheme abandoned. Renamed after the death of President Franklin Roosevelt in 1945, the little town evolved into an ordinary suburban community. But many of the severe, International-style homes and public buildings remain, reminders of a certain vision of the future that found appeal during the Depression's darkest days.

The Old Barracks were built in 1758 to house British troops fighting in the French and Indian wars. Formerly troops who were waiting out the winter for the next season's campaign had been billeted among New Jersey townspeople and farmers, but popular dissatisfaction with this practice (a resentment against being forced to quarter troops later made it into our Bill of Rights) led to the construction of army housing at five New Jersey locations. Rented out for other purposes by the legislature during the interim between the French and Indian and Revolutionary Wars, the barracks were activated again by the British when the rebellion broke out. When the war was over, the New Jersey legislature sold the barracks to private investors, who began fixing them up for use as civilian housing—one of the earliest instances of a type of "condo conversion" in a former institutional building. Throughout the nineteenth century the barracks and officers' quarters served one purpose after another, from tenements to schools to a home for widows. What remained of the complex (a portion was torn down in 1792) was finally purchased for preservation between 1902 and 1914, first by private groups and later by the state. The demolished section was rebuilt, the entire structure restored to its original appearance inside and out, and the Old Barracks Museum came into being.

Today's visitor to the Old Barracks is offered a rare view of what a soldier's life was like 200 years ago. Each of twenty-two 16-by-23-foot rooms, with their fireplaces (one to a room) and single doors, was home to up to fourteen men. Life in the nearby officers' quarters was, needless to say, a shade more pleasant.

Visitors meet role players in eighteenth-century dress, who portray Revolutionary War–era soldiers and camp women. In addition there's an orientation exhibit with a video introduction, changing historical exhibits, displays of original firearms, and dioramas of the Battle of Trenton.

The Old Barracks Museum, Barrack Street, Trenton 08608, (609) 396–1776, is open daily 10:00 A.M.–5:00 P.M. Admission is $2.00 for adults, $1.00 for senior citizens and students, and 50 cents for children under twelve.

Just minutes from Trenton's State House is a section of town called Chambersburg. Nicknamed *"Little Italy,"* it's a mecca for lovers of Italian food: Within one square mile there are numerous Italian restaurants—Amici Milano, Chianti's, Marsilio's, Rossi's—each with its own ambience and specialties. Perhaps the best way to choose is to wander about and inhale the wonderful aromas. For a brochure and map of Chambersburg and its restaurants, call (800) THE–BURG (in New Jersey only) or the Trenton Convention and Visitors Bureau at (609) 777–1771.

There are 366 polished black granite panels arranged in a circle at the *New Jersey Vietnam Veterans' Memorial*—one for each day of the year. Engraved on the dated panels are the names of the 1,553 New Jersey soldiers, marines, sailors, and airmen killed or reported missing in action on that date. At the center of the Memorial, under a red oak tree, three large bronze statues represent the more than 80,000 New Jerseyans who served in Southeast Asia. The Educational Center, which will use films, photographs, displays and other activities to put the Vietnam era into social, historical, political, and cultural context, is scheduled to open in May 1998.

New Jersey Vietnam Veterans' Memorial, 150 West State Street, Trenton, (609) 695–1854, is open at all times. Call for information on the Education Center.

Artifacts Gallery is a browser's dream—a treasure trove of antique and contemporary posters and prints, postcards, maps, sculpture, ephemera, collectibles, and memorabilia. The gallery is at 1025 South Broad Street, Trenton 08611, (609) 599–9081; closed Sunday and Monday. Hours are Tuesday and Friday 10:00 A.M.–5:30 P.M., Wednesday and Thursday 10:00 A.M.–8:00 P.M., and Saturday 10:00 A.M.–4:00 P.M.

In September 1921, 120 recruits reported to Sea Girt and began training under the watchful eye of Col. H. Norman Schwarzkopf, Stormin' Norman's father. Eighty-one passed the rigorous course and become New Jersey's first State Troopers. Their story and many others—including a fascinating, in-depth exhibit on the Lindbergh kidnapping—are told at the *New Jersey State Police Museum and Learning Center.*

Several of the exhibits here are interactive. In the Criminal Investigation area, visitors help a detective search a crime scene for evidence, analyze bullets and fibers under a microscope, and examine fingerprints. Part of the museum is housed in a 1934 log cabin that was originally used as a dormitory and classroom for new recruits. It now houses a transportation exhibit that includes a 1921 Harley Davidson motorcycle, a 1930 Buick State Police touring car, and a present-day cruiser car in which visitors can sit, activate the light bar, and listen to recordings of actual radio transmissions.

No Doubt It Was a Diner-Saur

*N*ew Jersey has two state animals: the horse, and Hadrosaurus foulkii, *a large dinosaur whose remains were found in the town of Haddonfield many years ago. Traces and skeletons of dinosaurs and other fossil animals have been uncovered at Fort Lee, and dinosaur tracks were found in the Triassic rock of the Palisades during construction of the George Washington Bridge. A model of hadrosaurus is on display at the State Museum in Trenton.*

The New Jersey State Police Museum and Learning Center, River Road (Route 175), West Trenton 08628, (609) 882–2000, ext. 6400, is open Monday through Saturday 10:00 A.M.–4:00 P.M. Admission is free.

Fred and Theresa Kuser began construction of their magnificent Queen Anne country home in 1888. They spared no expense. In addition to the mansion, a laundry house, barn, coachman's house, chicken house, windmill, shower house, and corn crib were constructed, as well as one of the finest clay tennis courts in New Jersey. Four years later the family finally sat down to its first dinner at ***Kuser Farm Mansion.***

A tour of the mansion includes a visit to the Delft Bedroom, whose fireplace has more than one hundred different Delft tiles, and the Kuser Farm Theatre/ Dining Room and Projection Room (the family helped finance the Fox Film Corporation, which later became 20th Century Fox). The intricately carved woodwork throughout the mansion was executed by German craftspersons on loan from the Peter Doelger Brewery in New York City (Ms. Kuser was the daughter of Mr. Doelger).

The Kuser Farm Mansion, 390 Newkirk Avenue, Hamilton 08610, (609) 890–3684, is open weekends, 11:00 A.M.–3:00 P.M. February through April; Thursday through Sunday 11:00 A.M.–3:00 P.M. May through November; and in December for special holiday events (call for information). The mansion is closed for the month of January. Last tour is at 2:30 P.M. Admission is free.

The 22-acre *Grounds for Sculpture,* on the site of the former New Jersey State Fairgrounds, showcases works by American and internationally known artists. Permanent pieces by artists such as Magdalena Abakanowicz, Marisol, and Anthony Coro and special exhibitions are displayed in two museums and on the lovely grounds. The al fresco cafe at the three-story gazebo overlooking the lotus pond is a delightful place to enjoy a box lunch, glass of wine, or espresso. There's also an indoor/outdoor restaurant in the new Domestic Arts Building museum.

The Grounds for Sculpture, 18 Fairgrounds Road, Hamilton 08619, (609) 586–0616, is open year-round, Friday, Saturday, and Sunday 10:00 A.M. to 4:00 P.M., and Tuesday through Thursday by appointment. Admission is free.

Bordentown, on the Delaware River just south of Trenton, is one of the oldest settlements of central New Jersey. The primary thrust of colonization in this part of the state was from the south (along the river) rather than from the New York Harbor area, as it was in the northern counties; consequently, the ethnic and cultural influences were English rather than Dutch and owed much to the Quaker society of early Philadelphia. The first settler of Bordentown was a Quaker shoemaker, Thomas Farnsworth, who arrived here from Burlington, New Jersey, in 1682. Farnsworth's property—it eventually totaled some 548 acres—was to form the core of the present-day community, and on it stand Bordentown's most important historic structures. Principal among these is **Bellevue,** also known as the **Gilder House** after its long association with the Gilder family of distinguished soldiers, authors, and musicians. Most likely built in the late 1780s and owned by the Gilders from the mid-nineteenth century until presented to the city of Bordentown in 1935, Bellevue is an expansive old home that demonstrates the organic growth of American practical architecture in the years immediately before and after 1800.

Three of the ground-floor rooms and four upper rooms of the Gilder House have been furnished by the Bordentown Historical Society with period furnishings and artwork. Among the most interesting are several pieces once owned by Emperor Napoleon's brother, Joseph Bonaparte, who, as deposed king of Naples and

Land Ho

*I*t is believed that the first white man to see the New Jersey shore was the Florentine navigator Giovanni da Verrazano, who sailed up the Atlantic Coast in 1524.

Spain, spent twenty years of comfortable exile at his Bordentown estate.

Bellevue, the Gilder House, on Crosswicks Street (near Route 130), Bordentown 08505, (609) 298–1740, is open for tours by special arrangement. For information contact the Bordentown Historical Society, 13 Crosswicks Street (P.O. Box 182), Bordentown 08505.

Within a block of the Gilder House is the *Clara Barton School,* a Bordentown landmark associated with the early career of the woman who was to found the American Red Cross. Barton's later humanitarian accomplishments tend to obscure the fact that she was instrumental in launching the concept of public education in New Jersey.

Before she came to Bordentown in 1852, the state's schools were mostly operated by religious institutions; those that were not generally assessed each student a fee that not everyone could afford. The only alternative was the poorly run, state-supported system of "pauper schools," usually conducted in an ill-trained teacher's home. In the year Clara Barton arrived, not one of Bordentown's seven schools occupied a town-owned building.

Clara Barton badgered the Bordentown school committee into reopening the old school building long used by the Quakers and other religious groups and briefly operated as a town school in 1839. In May 1852 she began teaching a class of six students; within a week the school's enrollment was fifty-five. By the following year there were three Bordentown schools, 600 pupils, and eight teachers. The town—and the state—needed no further convincing that a modern system of centralized public education could succeed in New Jersey as it was succeeding in Barton's native New England. Unfortunately Clara Barton wasn't around Bordentown for long to savor her triumph. Sidelined from teaching by the temporary failure of her voice, she was replaced by a new school principal.

Clara Barton's original schoolhouse in Bordentown was acquired by the city in 1920; it has since been restored to its original (at the time of her teaching) appearance. Located on Crosswicks Street near Farnsworth Avenue, it may be visited by arrangement with the Bordentown Historical Society. For details contact the Bordentown Historical Society at the address and telephone number listed above.

Burlington lies farther south along the river than Bordentown, and is older still. English Quakers arrived here as early as 1677; the settlement was incorporated as a township in 1693 and granted a city charter by King George II in 1734. By the time of the Revolution, Burlington was a center for pottery making and shipbuilding, and it enjoyed the status of a sea-trading port because of its easy river access to the open ocean.

Despite the fact that Burlington was chosen as the place where the New Jersey State Constitution would be written in 1776, the little city harbored a fair number of Tory sympathizers. One of them, a lawyer and mayor of Burlington, was John Lawrence. Lawrence left the United States for Canada at the close of the Revolution, but before he departed, his son James was born at what is now known as the *Lawrence House* on High Street.

James Lawrence's politics turned out to be quite a bit different than those of his father, as did his profession. Originally intended by his father to study law, young Lawrence was back in Burlington studying navigation by 1796 and two years later was a midshipman in the U.S. Navy. One year into the war with Great Britain, he was captain of the USS *Chesapeake*. It was during the *Chesapeake*'s losing engagement with the British ship *Shannon* that Captain Lawrence was mortally wounded, but before he died he uttered five of the most famous words in U.S. naval history: "Don't give up the ship!"

It isn't often that two Americans notable in entirely different fields turn out to have been born in adjacent houses, but this block of High Street in Burlington offers just such a coincidence. In 1798 the **Cooper House,** now the headquarters of the Burlington County Historical Society, was the birthplace of James Cooper (he added the middle name Fenimore as an adult) and his home for thirteen months before his parents packed up their large brood and headed for the upstate New York haunts with which the novelist became associated through works such as *The Deerslayer* and *The Last of the Mohicans*. He is remembered today, in the house that bears his name, with a collection of his works and an assortment of associated items. The house also contains a Bonaparte Room, furnished with items once belonging to Napoleon's brother Joseph Bonaparte during his Bordentown sojourn.

The oldest of the three houses that make up the Burlington County Historical Society's High Street Complex is the **Bard-Howe House,** built about 1743. Among the antiques on display at the house is a signed

The Cooper House, now the headquarters of the Burlington County Historical Society, was the birthplace of novelist James Fenimore Cooper.

clock, built by the accomplished local silversmith and clockmaker Isaac Pearson.

The Lawrence House is at 459 High Street, the Cooper House at 457, and the Bard-Howe House at 453. For information on hours during which each may be visited, as well as admission charges, contact the Burlington County Historical Society, 457 High Street, Burlington 08016, (609) 386–4773. The society's *Corson-Poley Center* exhibits an excellent collection of quilts, tall case clocks, and samplers, as well as examples of the J. H. Birch Company's jinrikishas (rickshaws).

Head on Route 524 toward Clarksburg to ***Horse Park of New Jersey at Stone Tavern, Inc.,*** the state's first major horse-show grounds. Activities here begin in late March and continue just about every weekend from May through October. Call for a calendar of events, (201) 337–7481 or (609) 758–8056; or write to P.O. Box 118, Allentown 08501.

Central Lowlands

Webbs' Mill Bog Cedar Swamp in the 27,298-acre Greenwood Wildlife Management Area is one of the few places in the state to hear—and possibly see—the endangered Pine Barrens tree frog, a tiny, bright green frog with lavender stripes. The best time to hear one is in the evening during the months of May and June. A boardwalk and trail run over a bog that's also home to the delicate pitcher plant and rare curly grass ferns. The area is also home to the endangered timber rattlesnakes: Although meetings are rare, if you do encounter one, just back away quietly. The swamp environment is a fragile one; be sure to stay on the boardwalk and trails.

Webbs' Mill Bog Cedar Swamp is on Country 539 south of Whiting. For more information, contact the New Jersey Division of Fish, Game and Wildlife, CN 400, Trenton 08625, (609) 259–7954.

After observing Germany's successful military use of zeppelins in World War I, the United States established the *Lakehurst Naval Air Station* and began making its own airships, or dirigibles. The popularity of dirigibles peaked in 1936, after the *Hindenburg* had completed ten successful commercial round-trips from Europe to Lakehurst, but in 1937 popularity crashed along with the dirigible after it exploded. Lakehurst Naval Air

Up in Flames

*T*he town of Lakehurst, long the site of the U.S. Navy's
Naval Air Engineering Center, has played a prominent role in
the development of lighter-than-air flight. But it wasn't an
American airship that figured in Lakehurst's most famous
event—it was the German luxury passenger dirigible
Hindenburg, which used the facility as a landing field in 1936
and 1937. On May 6, 1937, the Hindenburg caught fire while
approaching her mooring mast. The hydrogen-filled craft was
quickly consumed in flames, and thirty-six people were killed.
The disaster marked the end of lighter-than-air transatlantic
passenger service, even though airships filled with helium
instead of hydrogen would have been impervious to fire and
explosion. In the days of the Hindenburg, the United States
controlled world supplies of helium, which was considered a
strategic material and was withheld from the Nazi German
regime. In a way, those thirty-six unlucky airship travelers were
among the first victims of the gathering storm of World War II.

Station is now the **Naval Air Warfare Center at
Lakehurst,** and both the memorial plaque for the
Hindenburg and Historic Hangar #1 (the site of the first
international airport) are on the center's grounds.
Visitors must get a pass, which is good only for visiting
the Memorial Site, at the main gate, and must be
escorted through Hangar #1. *Cautions:* Ask before you
take photographs or your film may be confiscated. Call
ahead before you visit: Because the center is an active
Navy base, it might be closed for security purposes.

The Naval Air Warfare Center is on Route 547 (north of
Route 70), Lakehurst 98733, (732) 323–2620.

A trip back up the Delaware Valley to Trenton and due east across central New Jersey on I–195 will take you to **Historic Allaire Village** in **Allaire State Park.** Allaire Village was a company town, back in the days when the mining and smelting of bog iron was big business in these parts. James P. Allaire, a New York City brass founder, came here in 1822 to exploit this resource by means of an integrated mining, smelting, and forging operation. Within fifteen years he had created an entire community around his "Howell Works," with 400 employees, a free school, and even a stagecoach to Red Bank. Allaire's workers lived in substantial brick row houses, among the first examples of company housing in the United States. Among the products they turned out were kitchenware, stoves, screws, and flatirons.

The iron industry, however, was not destined to become a long-standing New Jersey staple. Once discovered, Pennsylvania anthracite coal became a cheaper fuel than local charcoal for smelting, and eventually large deposits of iron ore from the north-central Midwest made the mining of bog iron obsolete. After 1850 the village of Allaire became a ghost town. The fact that its buildings remain is due partly to the solidity of their brick construction and partly to the wise acquisition of the town and its environment by newspaperman Arthur Brisbane early in this century. For many years Monmouth County's Boy Scout organization used several of the buildings as headquarters and helped with restoration projects. In 1941 Brisbane's widow gave the village and much of the surrounding land to the state for use as a park, and restoration efforts continued. Putting an abandoned town back in shape after so long a period of disuse is a big job. Preservation and interpretation of the site continues under the directon of Allaire Village, Inc.

Among the sites to visit at Allaire today are the old carpenter and blacksmith shop, general store, and bakery; workers' houses and foreman's cottage; enameling furnace and casting-house stack; and the picturesque millpond, children only are allowed to fish.

As if a historic village weren't enough to make Allaire unique among New Jersey state parks, this is also the home of the *Pine Creek Railroad.* The steam-powered and diesel trains are operated by the New Jersey Museum of Transportation, and the rides last ten minutes.

Allaire State Park, on Route 524 (off I–195 exit 31B, and off Garden State Parkway exit 98), Allaire 07727, (732) 938–2371, is open daily year-round from dawn to dusk. An admission fee of $3.00 per car is charged only on weekends and holidays from Memorial Day through Labor Day. Historic Allaire Village buildings are open weekends May through October 10:00 A.M.–4:00 P.M. For museum information call (732) 938–2253. There is a separate charge for rides on the Pine Creek Railroad, which runs weekends in spring and fall, and daily, noon–4:00 P.M., during July and August. For railroad information call (732) 938–5524.

Collingwood Park Auction and Flea Market, with more than 600 indoor and outdoor tables, is a bargain hunter's paradise. Don't miss the antiques auction held Saturday nights in summer (preview starts at noon, bidding begins at 5:00 p.m.). There's also a slew of vendors selling fresh produce, flowers, baked goods, and food. The market, on Routes 33 and 34 (just ½ mile west of the Collingwood Circle) in Farmingdale 07727, (732) 938–7941, is open Friday and Saturday from 9:00 a.m. to 9:00 p.m., and Sunday 9:00 a.m. to 6:00 p.m.

Slightly to the northwest of Allaire is a state park dedicated in commemoration not of the long-term production of iron, but the short-term exchange of lead—in the form of musket balls. *Monmouth Battlefield State Park* came into being on June 28, 1978, the 200th anniversary of the Battle of Monmouth. The struggle that took place on that June day in 1778 was the longest of the entire Revolution, and the only one in which both supreme commanders—George Washington and Sir Harry Clinton—were involved against each other.

Among the tales of valor that emerged from the smoke and dust of Monmouth, one of the most enduring is that of Molly Pitcher. While her husband fought with the Continental army as a member of a cannon crew, Molly Pitcher carried water to thirsty soldiers during the heat of battle; when her husband was wounded, she herself took his place with the artillerymen. No one has been able to find exactly where Molly's well was, but just for the sake of heroic tradition, if not accuracy, a reproduction has been set up on Route 522 in the 1,520-acre park. Other park features include a Visitor's Center and a marked footpath through the battlefield.

Another important park attraction is the *Craig House*, a 1710 farmstead occupied at the time of the battle by the family of John Craig, paymaster for the local patriot militia. Craig fought at the Battle of Monmouth, and his wife, children, and two slaves left their home when it was apparent that the British were approaching the vicinity. The enemy found Mrs. Craig's silver (hidden in the bottom of the well, which is the first place we would look if we were pillaging enemy territory), and used the house to treat their wounded. The place survived the battle intact and has now been restored to its Revolutionary-era appearance. The four-room Craig House, with its massive kitchen hearth and three smaller fireplaces, offers a good look at how eighteenth-century women lived when they weren't fighting off His Majesty's army or throwing their silver down the well.

Monmouth Battlefield State Park, accessible via Route 9 or Route 33, Freehold 07728, (908) 462–9616, is open daily during daylight hours. The Visitor's Center is open daily, 8:00 A.M.– 4:00 P.M. Because the Craig House is staffed by volunteers, the hours it is open are erratic. Call for information. There is no admission fee.

You never know what you'll find at the **Monmouth Museum,** founded in 1963 as a "Museum of Ideas." Exhibitions on art, science, nature, culture, and history change constantly. Art and artifacts for the exhibits are borrowed from the nation's leading museums, galleries, and private collections. Kids can participate in a variety of hands-on activities at the Becker Children's Wing,

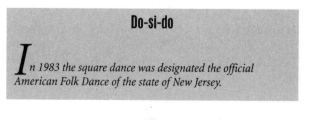

Do-si-do

*I*n 1983 the square dance was designated the official American Folk Dance of the state of New Jersey.

where the exhibitions, which change every two years, complement the curriculum of the local schools.

Monmouth Museum, Newman Springs Road, P.O. Box 359, Lincroft 07738, (732) 747–2266, is open Tuesday and Thursday 2:00–4:30 P.M.; Friday and Saturday 10:00 A.M.–4:30 P.M.; and Sunday 1:00–5:00 P.M. Admission is $4.00. Children two and under are free.

Until such time as Paterson renames its East Side after Allen Ginsberg or Rutherford comes through with a William Carlos Williams neighborhood, Matawan will remain the only New Jersey community with a section named after an American poet. The poet is Philip Freneau, known as the "Poet of the American Revolution" because of his biting anti-British satirical verse. Freneau lived on an estate called Mount Pleasant in Middletown Point, as Matawan was then called. After his house burned down in 1818, he spent his last fourteen years with relatives near Freehold. Having been out drinking in Freehold village one December night in 1832, the eighty-year-old poet got lost while walking home and died of exposure in a bog. He was buried in the family plot on his old estate, in what is now the built-up Freneau section of Matawan. The *Freneau Gravesite,* which may still be visited, is at the end of a short, tree-lined drive on the left side of Route 79, about a mile south of Freneau Center. The grave is marked by a marble shaft, which stands within a small fenced enclosure.

Has it always been your dream to pilot an AT-6 fighter plane? How about flying low and slow over the Verrazano-Narrows Bridge and the Statue of Liberty in an open-cockpit biplane? *Biplane Adventure Tours*

Take a ride in an open-cockpit biplane
with Biplane Adventure Tours Ltd.

Ltd. offers a variety of such tours and rides. The biplane rides last from fifteen minutes ($70 for two persons) to an hour and twenty minutes ($350 for two persons) and are given in one of their original antique biplanes, which include a 1943 Stearman biplane and a 1940 Waco UPF-7. The AT6/SNJ, a World War II advanced trainer and fighter, was equipped with bombs and guns in 1944. It has a full-swivel rear gunner's seat and airshow smoke and is equipped with parachutes, military flight suits, and dual controls so that you can co-pilot it yourself (half hour, $230; full hour, $399).

Biplane Adventure Tours Ltd., Old Bridge Airport (adjacent to Raceway Park), Pension Road, Englishtown, (732) 446–1300, is open 9:00 A.M.–5:00 P.M. Wednesday through Sunday from the third weekend in April through October. Advance reservations are highly recommended.

The Name Game

Rutgers, New Jersey's state university, was chartered in 1766 and ranks as the eighth oldest institution of higher learning in the British American colonies. But the university, which has its main campus in New Brunswick, wasn't always called Rutgers. It was originally called Queen's College, in honor of George III's consort Queen Charlotte, and was renamed in 1825 after a prosperous local citizen, Colonel Henry Rutgers. Hoping that the colonel would come to the aid of the financially strapped college, the administration effected the name change in his honor before actually receiving a contribution. Rutgers did loosen his purse strings, eventually donating more than $5,000 to the school.

Constantine's doesn't look like much from the outside, but true gourmets know it's what's cooking that counts. And delicious things are cooking in chef Roberto Capasso's kitchen: creations like chunks of fresh lobster on a raft of goat cheese in a phyllo dough surrounded by a puddle of leek, basil, and saffron cream sauce. And boneless chicken breast stuffed with spinach and pine nuts with a Cabernet and tarragon mustard sauce. Or a favorite, the grilled veal chop served with porcini-mushroom sauce. The restaurant, at 1012 Amboy Avenue, Edison, (732) 225–0540, is open for lunch Monday through Friday, and dinner Monday through Saturday. BYOB.

The Jane Voorhees **Zimmerli Art Museum** on the New Brunswick campus of Rutgers University houses the school's collection of more than 35,000 works of art. The museum's major concentrations are in nineteenth-century French graphics, Russian and Soviet art, twentieth-century American art, and contemporary American printmaking. The collection also includes ancient art and European art of the fifteenth through nineteenth centuries, pre-Columbian ceramics, and designs for American stained glass. The Zimmerli incorporates the International Center for Japonisme and presents related art in the Kusakabe-Griffis Japonisme Gallery. A special gallery features the extensive Rutgers Collection of Illustrations for Children's Literature. At the entry level of the modern museum building are special exhibition galleries, the George Riabov Collection of Russian Art, a cafe, and a gift shop; works from the permanent collection are exhibited on the lower level.

The Zimmerli Art Museum, Rutgers University, George and Hamilton Streets, New Brunswick 08903, (732) 932–7237, is open weekdays except Mondays 10:00 A.M.–4:30 P.M., and on weekends noon–5:00 P.M. The museum is closed on major holidays, Mondays and Tuesdays in July, and all of August. Admission is free.

"Life is uncertain. Eat dessert first!" cautions the menu at *Old Man Rafferty's.* To make sure you heed the warning, Rafferty's offers more than four dozen sweets from which to choose. The restaurant, near Rutgers University, also serves moderately priced steaks, sandwiches, salads, and a terrific selection of wines and beers. The restaurant, at 106 Albany Street, New Brunswick 08903, (732) 846–6153, is open Monday through Thursday 11:30 A.M.–11:00 P.M.; Friday 11:30 A.M.–midnight; Saturday noon–midnight; and Sunday noon–10:00 P.M.

In East Millstone there is a tract of natural land that is a good deal smaller than the Great Swamp but no less remarkable for having survived in primeval condition right down into our own time. This is the **Hutcheson Memorial Forest,** 400 acres of woods and fields maintained by the Department of Ecology, Evolution, and Natural Resources at Rutgers University.

At the core of the Hutcheson tract (it's named after William L. Hutcheson, a past president of the United Brotherhood of Carpenters and Joiners, which was instrumental in securing the forest preservation) is sixty-four-acre Mettler's Woods, believed to be the only uncut upland forest in New Jersey. *Uncut* means that throughout three and a half centuries, while the vast forests of the ever-more-populous Northeast fell for cordwood, for buildings, and to clear land for agriculture, this tiny tract escaped the axe. This is not to say that the elements haven't taken their toll; fire, wind, and insects interfere in the lives of all primeval forests. But there has never been any timber harvesting or soil cultivation here. The living white oak trees in Mettler's Woods average 235 years in age, whereas some of the trees that have died within the past twenty years have been up to 350 years old.

Mettler's Woods is surrounded by over 300 acres of younger forest, consisting of second growth over land that was previously cultivated and logged. This adjacent forest helps researchers understand the difference between untouched climax growth and the far more prevalent reestablished forest; also, it provides a welcome buffer for the primeval woods within.

The Hutcheson Memorial Forest is open to visitors on selected Sundays throughout the year, by scheduled tour only. Reservations aren't necessary for individuals and groups smaller than ten. For schedules and directions to the forest, contact the Director, Hutcheson Memorial Forest, Department of Ecology, Evolution, and Natural Resources, Rutgers University, P.O. Box 1059, Piscataway 08855, (201) 932–2075. There is no charge for tours.

The aptly named *Pillars B&B*, a restored Georgian Revival mansion, boasts—count 'em—fourteen pillars surrounding its front porch. Set on an acre of land in the town's Van Wyck Brooks Historic District, the house is surrounded by wildflowers, flowering trees, rhododendrons and azaleas. A circular staircase winds up 3 stories to a stained-glass skylight and leads to five beautifully furnished rooms, each with private bath (one has a fireplace). Refreshments, including wine and home-baked cookies, are served hearthside in the Music Room each afternoon and evening.

Rooms at the Pillars B&B, 922 Central Avenue, Plainfield 07060, (888)–PILLARS, range in price from $69 to $89. Children under the age of two and over the age of twelve are welcome. The innkeepers' cairn terrier, Mac, presides over the mansion.

PLACES TO STAY
IN CENTRAL NEW JERSEY

AMBER HOUSE
66 Leigh Way, Clinton 08809;
(908) 735–7881

BRUNSWICK HOTEL
10 Livingston Avenue, New
Brunswick 08901;
(732) 214–1717

CABBAGE ROSE INN
162 Main Street, Flemington
08822; (908) 788–0247

HOLLY THORN HOUSE
143 Readington Road, White
House Station 08889;
(908) 534–1616

HYATT REGENCY PRINCETON
102 Carnegie Center, Princeton
08540; (800) 233–1234 or
(609) 987–1234;
fax (609) 987–2584

JERICA HILL INN
96 Broad Street, Flemington
08822; (908) 782–8234

THE NATIONAL HOTEL
31 Race Street, Frenchtown
08825; (908) 996–4871

SEVEN SPRINGS FARM B&B
14 Perryville Road, Pittstown
08867; (908) 735–7675

PLACES TO EAT
IN CENTRAL NEW JERSEY

ACACIA
2637 Main Street, Route 206,
Lawrenceville; (609) 895–9885

THE FERRY HOUSE
21 Ferry Street, Lambertville;
(609) 397–9222

**FORK'S INN RESTAURANT
AND MARINA**
4800 Pleasant Mills Road,
Sweetwater; (609) 567–8889

FROG AND THE PEACH
Hiram Square, New Brunswick;
(732) 846–3216

GIRAFE
95 Morristown Road,
(Route 202), Basking Ridge;
(908) 221–0017

HARVEST MOON INN
1039 Old York Road, Ringoes;
(908) 806–6020

IL POMODORO
1 West High Street, Somerville;
(908) 526–4466

KAKONO
Marketplace Shopping Center,
Route 27, Franklin Park;
(732) 821–8822

LA PETITE ROSE
Westfield Inn, 431 North Avenue,
Westfield; (908) 232–1680

THE LITTLE KRAUT
115 Oakland Street, Red Bank;
(732) 842–4830
(German cuisine)

PALACE OF ASIA
400 Mercer Mall, Route 1,
Lawrenceville; (609) 987–0606
(Indian cuisine)

SCALINI FEDELI
63 Main Street, Chatham;
(973) 701–9200

SOMERSET & MAIN
215 Main Street, Whitehouse
Station; (908) 534–5055

STAGE HOUSE INN
366 Park Avenue, Scotch Plains;
(732) 322–4224

STAGE LEFT: AN AMERICAN CAFE
5 Livingston Avenue, New
Brunswick; (732) 828–3796

OTHER ATTRACTIONS
IN CENTRAL NEW JERSEY

BEVERLY NATIONAL CEMETERY
Bridgeboro Road, Beverly 08010;
(609) 877–5460

ENGLISHTOWN AUCTION
90 Wilson Avenue, Englishtown
07726; (732) 446–9644

GABRIEL DAVIES TAVERN
Fourth and Floodgate Roads,
P.O. Box 68, Glendora 08012;
(609) 939–2699

GARDEN STATE DISCOVERY MUSEUM
16 North Springdale Road,
Cherry Hill 08003;
(609) 424–6516

HERITAGE GLASS MUSEUM
High and Center Streets,
Glassboro 08028; (609)
881–7468

LAKEHURST HISTORICAL SOCIETY
Old Street John's Church, 300
Center Street, Lakehurst 08733;
(732) 657–8864

LAWRENCEVILLE HISTORIC HOMES
Lawrenceville 08648; (609)
844–7000

LONGSTREET FARM
Holmdel Park, Longstreet Road,
Holmdel 07733; (732) 946–3758

MONMOUTH BATTLEFIELD, MONMOUTH BATTLEFIELD STATE PARK
(off Route 33), Manalapan
07726; (732) 462–9616

NEW JERSEY STATE MUSEUM
CN 530, 205 West State Street,
Trenton 08625; (609) 292–6308/
292–6464

RED BANK BATTLEFIELD
100 Hessian Avenue, National Park 08063; (609) 853–5120

SMITHVILLE MANSION
Smithville Road, P.O. Box 6000, Easthampton 08060; (609) 265–5068/261–3780

STATE HOUSE
CN 068, 125 West State Street, Trenton 08625; (609) 677–2705

THOMAS H. KEAN NEW JERSEY STATE AQUARIUM
1 Riverside Drive, Camden 08103; (609) 365–3300/ 365–8332

WASHINGTON CROSSING STATE PARK
355 Washington Crossing–Pennington Road, (Route 546), Titusville 08560; (609) 737–0623

Selected Regional Information Centers, Chambers of Commerce, and Visitor Centers in Central New Jersey

Greater Bordentown Chamber of Commerce, *P.O. Box 65, Bordentown 08505, (609) 298–7774*

Trenton Convention and Visitors Bureau, *CN 206, Lafayette and Barrack Streets, Trenton 08625, (609) 777–1771*

The Shore

At one time or another, nearly everybody in New Jersey has gone "Down the Shore." Little kids have enjoyed the rides at Asbury Park, and big kids have cruised the boardwalk at Seaside Heights; the rich have gone to Deal and Allenhurst, whereas the not-so-rich take their sun at Lavallette or Ortley Beach. Methodists flock to camp meeting at teetotaling Ocean Grove, high rollers hit the blackjack tables at "A.C.," and surfers search for the perfect Jersey wave at—where else?— Surf City (there were never "two girls for every boy" there, regardless of what the song said). And some people are even discovering what savvy summer travelers knew a hundred years ago, by heading for the Victorian guest houses of Cape May as an alternative to four-digit weekends on certain New England islands. For that matter even a fair number of people who *aren't* from the Garden State go to the Jersey Shore (and not just Atlantic City), simply because it *is* one of the finest ocean beaches in the world's temperate zones, period.

So what can there be to learn about the Shore? Plenty, if you want to come in out of the sun for a bit and look behind the slot machines and sausage-and-pepper stands. The Jersey Shore has a rich history of settlers and shipwrecks, lighthouses and naval engagements, and there's the land itself—barrier dunes, salt marshes, and even a holly forest. Much of the region would surprise even a lifelong visitor. Like the urban northeastern corner of New Jersey, the Shore is a part of the state that people think they know and few really try to discover.

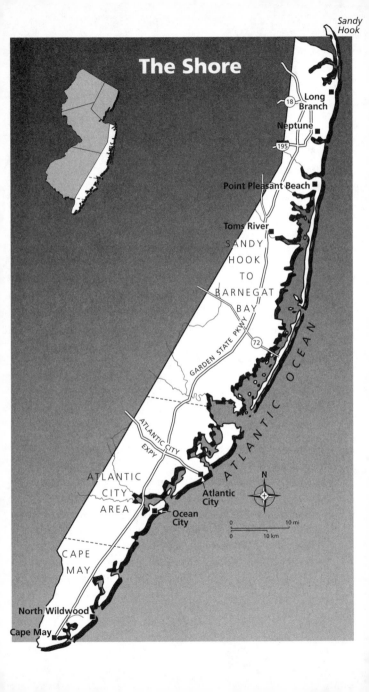

The Shore

Sandy Hook

Long Branch

Neptune

Point Pleasant Beach

Toms River

SANDY HOOK TO BARNEGAT BAY

GARDEN STATE PKWY

72

ATLANTIC OCEAN

ATLANTIC CITY EXPY

ATLANTIC CITY AREA

Atlantic City

Ocean City

CAPE MAY

North Wildwood

Cape May

N

0   10 mi
0   10 km

The Shore's Top Picks

Gateway National Recreation Area (Sandy Hook)

Twin Lights

Ocean Grove

Co-op Seafood

Floyd L. Moreland Historic Dentzel/Looff Carousel

Maritime Museum

Popcorn Park Zoo

Albert Music Hall

Green Gables Inn & Restaurant

Edwin B. Forsythe National Wildlife Refuge

Barnegat Bay Decoy and Baymen's Museum

Noyes Museum of Art

Marine Mammal Stranding Center and Sea Life Museum

Lucy the Elephant

Somers Mansion

Ocean City Historical Museum

Stone Harbor Bird Sanctuary

The Wetlands Institute

Leaming's Run Gardens and Colonial Farm

Cape May County Zoo

Cape May

Emlen Physick Estate

Angel of the Sea

Cape May Lighthouse

Note: The orientation in this chapter is from north to south; from Sandy Hook to Barnegat Bay, through the Atlantic City area, and down to Cape May.

Sandy Hook to Barnegat Bay

The northernmost reach of the Jersey Shore proper is the curving finger of land called *Sandy Hook.* Saved from development for nearly two centuries because of its status as a federal military reserve, Sandy Hook is now a unit of the *Gateway National Recreation Area,* other sections of which occupy shoreline stretches of Staten Island and Long Island.

The oldest structure on Sandy Hook is the 1764 *Sandy Hook Light,* visible 19 miles out at sea. The United States government acquired all of Sandy Hook in 1817, and the first permanent fort construction started in 1859. But construction was suspended eight years later and the fort was never completed. In 1895, shore batteries and attendant facilities were officially named *Fort Hancock.* The fort was deactivated in 1974, and, as surplus government property, it became part of Gateway.

Although a number of the Fort Hancock buildings have been adaptively reused and incorporated into Gateway's interpretive program, most of Sandy Hook is of interest because of the natural environment. The areas along the eastern Atlantic Ocean face of the peninsula are mostly primary and secondary dunes, but you don't have to go very far inland to find dense thickets of bayberry, beach plum, and even random clumps of prickly pear cactus (there's also poison ivy, so be careful). The most unusual

Authors' Favorite Attractions at the Shore

Barnegat Bay Decoy and Baymen's Museum
Cape May
Leaming's Run Gardens and Colonial Farm
Lucy the Elephant
Marine Mammal Stranding Center and Sea Life Museum
Ocean Grove
Popcorn Park Zoo

Top Annual Events at the Shore

Note: Schedules may vary; call ahead.

Wildwood International Kite Festival, Wildwood; May;
(609) 523–0100

New Jersey Seafood Festival, Belmar; June; (732) 681–2900

America's Playground Beach Fest, Atlantic City; June;
(609) 641–7811

New Jersey Offshore Powerboat Race, Point Pleasant Beach; July;
(732) 899–2424

Harbor Music Fest and Atlantic City Ocean Marathon Swim,
Atlantic City; August; (609) 348–8059

Street Rod Weekend, Ocean City; September; (609) 525–9300

Clownfest, Seaside Heights; September; (732) 741–4459

Wings 'n Water Festival, Wetlands Institute, Stone Harbor;
September; (609) 369–1211

Old Time Barnegat Bay Decoy and Gunning Show, Tuckerton;
September; (609) 971–3085

Miss America Pageant, Atlantic City; September; (609) 345–7571

Victorian Week, Cape May; October; (609) 884–5404

America's Great Halloween Experience, The Wildwoods;
November; (609) 729–3700, ext. 700

aspect of Sandy Hook, to most first-time visitors, is the holly forest. Holly does well in sandy soil, and its leaves are tough enough to withstand salt breezes.

The **Gateway Sandy Hook Unit Visitors' Center** is located on Spermaceti Cove (2 miles beyond the entrance gate) in a building that at one time housed the all-important U.S. Life Saving Service. Maps of all the area's self-guided nature trails are available here, as are details of organized programs and guided nature and history tours.

Behind the Visitors' Center is **Sandy Hook Museum.** Formerly a guardhouse and jail, this 1899 structure houses exhibits concentrating on the history of America's oldest operating lighthouse, which stands only a few yards away.

The Sandy Hook Unit of Gateway National Recreation Area, off Route 36, Highlands 07732, (732) 872–0115, is open daily throughout the year during daylight hours. The Visitors' Center is open daily 10:00 A.M.–5:00 P.M.; closed Thanksgiving, Christmas, and New Year's Day. The museum is open weekends 1:00–5:00 P.M. throughout the year and daily during July and August. There is a

The State Shell

*I*n 1995 the knobbed whelk, also known as Busycon carica gmelin or the conch shell, was designated the official state shell. The large, pear-shaped, yellowish-gray shell can be found along the state's beaches.

$4.00 weekday ($5.00 weekend) charge for parking in beach parking areas between Memorial Day weekend and Labor Day. Visitors' Center and Fort Hancock parking area are free.

As you approach Sandy Hook from the mainland, it's impossible not to notice the massive stone towers of a double lighthouse that dominates the bluff of the Highlands. These are **Twin Lights,** also known as the **Navesink Light Station,** decommissioned in 1949 and now maintained as a New Jersey State Park.

Twin Lights was once one of the five major lighthouse installations that dotted the dangerous 127-mile-long New Jersey coast. Built in 1862 to replace a pair of stone light towers that had stood on the Highlands since 1828, the north and south towers of Navesink each held beacons to inform mariners of the approach to land.

The south tower held a light of the "first order," indicating simply that landfall was at hand. The north tower was equipped with a "second order" light, indicating a headland and the approach to a bay—in this case, the lower bay of New York harbor. As a first-order light, the south-tower installation was always the brighter of the two, and in 1898 it became the brightest in the United States. The Statue of Liberty is tradi-tionally regarded as the first sight of America for passengers on incoming ships, but to any seaman or traveler who approached the coast at night, Twin Lights on the Navesink heralded the New World.

Although a small blinking beacon is still lit in the north tower between dusk and dawn, the south tower is dark. Its giant Fresnel lens, at one time so blindingly powerful that the west-facing windows of the tower had to be paneled over lest the entire countryside be floodlit, is on exhibit today at ground level, in what was formerly the lighthouse's power-generating station. The clockwork mechanism that operated the light is also on exhibit.

A visit to the **Twin Lights Museum** will reveal more than lighthouse technology. Here also are collections of memorabilia that relate to the Life Saving Service and to the work of Guglielmo Marconi, inventor of wireless telegraphy. It was at Navesink, in 1899, that Marconi gave his first demonstrations of wireless transmission. In September he reported on the progress of Spanish-American War hero Admiral Dewey's triumphal fleet off the Jersey coast; a month later, his wireless wizardry allowed the *New York Herald* to receive instantaneous news of the America's Cup races near Sandy Hook.

Before or after visiting the museum, climb the sixty-four steps to the top of the north tower, 246 feet above sea level. (The north tower is open during museum hours; the south tower only occasionally.)

Twin Lights Historic Site State Park, Lighthouse Road (off Route 36), Highlands 07732, (732) 872–1814, is open Labor Day to Memorial Day, Wednesday through Sunday 10:00 A.M.–5:00 P.M.; Memorial Day to Labor Day open daily 10:00 A.M.–5:00 P.M. The grounds are open until sunset. Admission is free.

If you wish a more sedate form of sightseeing than scampering around and up lighthouses, consider a ride on the **Sandy Hook Lady,** an authentic, 85-foot paddle wheeler that leaves from Atlantic Highlands Harbor and cruises the historic Shrewsbury and Navesink Rivers.

The *Lady* offers luncheon, dinner, and Sunday-brunch cruises as well as regular sightseeing excursions.

Sandy Hook Lady, Atlantic Highlands Harbor (mailing address: 121A East Highland Avenue, Atlantic Highlands 07716), (908) 291–4354, operates daily from Mother's Day through October.

Do you want to learn about spyhops? or flipper flops? Sign on for a whale-watch cruise aboard one of ***TNT Hydrolines, Inc.****'s* high-speed catamarans. The cruises last four to five hours (depending on whale activity) and leave weekends at 9:00 A.M. from Conner's Hotel in Atlantic Highlands, from December through March. During the Mets baseball season, from May through September, TNT runs a ferry from the hotel to Shea Stadium and back at the end of the game. Reservations for the whale watch and stadium ferry are required.

TNT Hydrolines, Inc. is at Two First Avenue, Atlantic Highlands 07716, (800) BOAT–RIDE or (732) 872–BOAT. Call for fare information.

The often-long wait for a table at ***Doris & Ed's*** gives credibility to its reputation as one of the Shore's best seafood restaurants. Although dress is casual, this isn't a casual fish house. In addition to fried seafood platters, the kitchen turns out finely prepared specialties such as bouillabaisse, tuna carpaccio, and lobster stuffed with fresh lump crabmeat. There's also a large selection of oysters from around the world, and an excellent wine list. Reservations are not accepted; 348 Shore Road, Highlands 07732, (732) 872–1565. Open for dinner late February through December, nightly except Monday (opens Sunday at 3:00 P.M.).

Next door to Asbury Park is an entire town entered in the National Register of Historic Places. *Ocean Grove,* which has one of the largest assemblages of authentic Victorian architecture in the United States, was founded in 1869 for The Ocean Grove Camp Meeting Association by Dr. William B. Osborn. He chose this one square mile because it had the highest beach and the best grove of trees around—and no mosquitoes.

When the first camp meeting was held in 1870, the faithful erected tents in which to live. Camp meetings are still held every summer, and today 114 tent structures ring the 6,000-seat Great Auditorium in Auditorium Square. Each July the Historical Society of Ocean Grove includes one or two of the tents on the tour it offers (which also includes seven Victorian houses). Contact the Historical Society of Ocean Grove, P.O. Box 446, Ocean Grove 07756, (732) 774–1869. Events are held in the auditorium throughout the summer months. If you're fortunate enough to be in the area Wednesday at 7:00 P.M. or Saturday at 4:00 P.M., don't miss the concerts on the world-famous Hope-Jones organ. A free-will offering is requested. Call (908) 775–0035 for information.

Don't miss a visit to *Centennial Cottage,* a completely restored and furnished vacation home built in 1874. Also operated by the Historical Society of Ocean Grove, the cottage, at the corner of Central Avenue and McClintock Street, is open daily except Sundays, in July and August, 10:00 A.M.–noon and 2:00–4:00 P.M. Admission is $1.00 for adults and 25 cents for children.

Want to have a picnic on the uncommercialized boardwalk or the beach? Stop in at the tiny *Raspberry*

Cafe at 58 Main Street, (732) 988–0833. Their soups, breads, and salads are terrific. If you're ready to spend the night, the small Victorian *Pine Tree Inn* has charming rooms and serves a scrumptious continental-plus breakfast each morning on the porch, which overlooks the Atlantic. The inn is at 10 Main Avenue, Ocean Grove 07756, (908) 775–3264. If you plan to dine at a restaurant in town, keep in mind that Ocean Grove is "dry"—no alcohol is served or allowed.

Down the road apiece in Spring Lake is another splendid Victorian B&B—the *Normandy Inn.* Built as a private residence in 1888, the oceanfront inn serves guests a huge country breakfast and then lends them bicycles so that they can work off the calories with a ride on the town's boardwalk. The inn is at 21 Tuttle Avenue, Spring Lake 07762, (732) 449–7172.

Ready for a "cuppa"? Stop in at *Radishes to Roses* for afternoon tea, served with scones, finger sandwiches, and assorted desserts every day but Tuesday from 2:30 to 5:30 P.M. The charming tearoom has a cozy ambiance and lots of tea-related goodies for sale. Because it *is* cozy, reservations are recommended; 508 Washington Boulevard, Sea Girt 08750, (732) 449–4442.

Up to 10 million pounds of fresh fish a year are caught by fishermen from Point Pleasant Beach, making it the third-largest fishing port in New Jersey. The best place to sample the wares is at the eighteen-member retail market/take-out restaurant *Co-op Seafood,* which serves up some of the freshest and most delicious fare on the coast. House specials include shrimp scampi, fish and fries, and the combination plate—a medley of crab

Early Resort Development

*N*ew Jersey has long been famous for its 120-mile-long ocean shoreline—but the seashore, where Indians fished and harvested salt from dried tidal pools, was one of the last places early colonists cared to settle. The barrier beach islands offered few decent harbors, and the mosquitoes were ferocious.

The story of Lavalette, a popular middle-class resort community with a steady year-round population, is typical. Developers started making their pitch in the 1870s, issuing a prospectus that praised the local crabbing and bluefishing. The promoters used a nineteenth-century version of today's condo timeshare come-on: They'd charter a train to Toms River, 7 miles away on the mainland, hire a sailing yacht, and bring prospects across Barnegat Bay for a picnic on the Lavalette beach. After 1881, the railroad extended across the bay right into Lavalette, and the resort boom began in earnest.

cakes, fish fillets, ocean scallops, and shrimp. The Co-op offers a free tour of the facility, which includes a trip to the docks to watch the unloading of the day's catch. The tour lasts forty-five minutes to an hour, and reservations are required. Co-op Seafood, Channel Drive in Point Pleasant Beach, (732) 899–2211, is open year-round; winter months, 9:30 A.M.–6:00 P.M., closed Mondays; summer months, 9:30 A.M.–8:00 P.M.

Wednesday evenings in summer, pack a picnic and a chair and head down to *Jenkinson's Pavilion* at Point Pleasant Beach for the free live classical and Broadway summer concerts. For the best seats, get there before 5:00 P.M. Call (732) 899–0902 for information.

Built in 1914 as a private summer home, the three-storied, pillared *Bay Head Gables* has been accommodating Ocean County guests for more than fifty years. Attributed to noted architect Stanford White, the the Georgian Revival mansion features a 150-foot wraparound porch, manicured lawns, and flower gardens. Each of the elegantly appointed guest rooms has its own bath and is air-conditioned. Five have ocean views, including the Contemporary Room, with a private patio. A five-course breakfast is included in the rate. Among the numerous artworks that decorate the walls is a collection of serigraphs by Thomas McKnight.

Bay Head Gables, 200 Maine Avenue, Bay Head 08742, (800) 984–9536 or (732) 892–9844, is open nightly from March through January 1, and generally on weekends in winter (but call in advance). Rates range from $95 to $195. The nonsmoking inn is not suitable for small children.

South of Point Pleasant there are, in effect, two Jersey shores—the narrow strip of barrier beach that actually faces the Atlantic, and the marshy inner shore that fronts the Intracoastal Waterway and Barnegat Bay. The beach resorts are clustered out on the sandy ocean shore. Head south along the beach road, Route 35, to Seaside Heights' Casino Pier for a ride on one of the country's finest hand-carved wooden carousels. The *Floyd L. Moreland Historic Dentzel/Looff Carousel,* more than eighty years old, is one of approximately 130 carousels left in the United States—and the number is diminishing rapidly, as each year some are destroyed by the elements and others are dismantled and sold off to collectors and museums. Music at the Seaside Heights carousel is provided by New Jersey's only continuously operating Wurlitzer Military Band Organ, which plays by means of a pneumatic system generated by leather bellows. The notes are activated by perforated music rolls like those of a player piano. The fifty-eight animals—thirty-six of which move up and down—were carved by William Dentzel and Charles Looff. Fifteen of the eighteen paintings on the "header," at the top of the center casings, are the original ones.

The Carousel at Casino Pier, Seaside Heights 08751, (732) 830–4183, is open daily during summer, 10:00 A.M.–midnight, and on weekends and holidays all year from noon until early evening. A small fee is charged for rides.

There are few more beautiful—and uncrowded—spots to be on an early morning than **Island Beach State Park**, a 3,002-acre paradise of white, sandy beach, windswept dunes, wetlands, sea grass, and nature trails that stretches for 10 miles between the ocean and Barnegat Bay. For a wonderful view of Barnegat Light, across Barnegat Inlet at the northern tip of Long Beach Island, drive to the end of the island and hike for 1½ miles to the southern tip of the peninsula.

During the summer, naturalists lead canoe and kayak trips through the tidal marshes to observe nesting ospreys, falcons, and shorebirds. For a bird's-eye view of the state's largest osprey colony, which thrives on the Sedge Islands—marshy masses of land in Barnegat Bay—park at lot A20 and hike a short distance to the Spizzle Creek Bird Observation Blind. The park is a horticulturist's as well as an ornithologist's dream: More than 300 plants have been identified here, and the grounds include the state's largest expanses of beach heather.

Island Beach State Park, Route 35 (mailing address: P.O. Box 37, Seaside Park 08752), (732) 793–0506, is open daily year-round. From Memorial Day to Labor Day, admission is $6.00 per vehicle Monday through Friday; $7.00 on weekends. The rest of the year admission is $4.00 per vehicle.

Back on the mainland in Toms River is a museum dedicated to the preservation of New Jersey's maritime heritage, with emphasis on the Barnegat Bay area. A number of boat types were developed and built in the area to allow fishermen access to the area's shallow estuaries and bays. The **Maritime Museum,** operated by Toms River Seaport Society, displays a number of these craft, including the *Sheldrake,* a 12-foot "sneakbox," in which the late F. Slade Dale cruised from Bay Head to New York and then on to Florida in 1925 (the Barnegat

An Unexpected Port of Call

*O*n September 8, 1934, the liner Morro Castle *caught fire off the New Jersey coast on the return leg of a New York to Havana cruise. The blaze took the lives of 134 passengers and crew, and left the powerless ship to the mercy of the waves and wind. The smoldering hulk soon grounded only a few hundred yards off the beach at Asbury Park, where it became a macabre tourist attraction for several months before being towed away and scrapped.*

Bay sneakbox, named for its ability to sneak up quietly on waterfowl, was invented by Hazelton Seaman of West Creek; historians credit the sneakbox as possibly the only boat designed in the United States without any Old World ancestors). Their growing collection, which now numbers thirty, includes a lifesaving surf rowboat, a Barnegat Bay garvey, and a Hankins rowing skiff. The two-story museum, headquartered in an 1868 carriage house, also displays numerous artifacts associated with the area's marine history.

The Maritime Museum, on the corner of Hooper Avenue and Water Street, Toms River 08754, (732) 349–9209, is open Tuesdays and Saturdays 10:00 A.M.–2:00 P.M. Donations are welcome.

If your interests tend to the celestial, visit the ***Robert J. Novins Planetarium*** at Ocean County College. The planetarium offers a number of programs, including Messengers from the Dark, Martian Mysteries, Images of the Universe, A Sky for all Seasons, and a Young Children's Show for children ages four to six.

Call the Robert J. Novins Planetarium, Ocean County College, College Drive, Toms River 08754, (732) 255–0342, for recorded show information. The planetarium office, (908) 255–0343, is open weekdays 9:30 A.M.–4:00 P.M. Admission fees are $5.00 for adults, $3.00 for children ages six to twelve, and $3.50 for all seats for the young children's show. Children under six are not admitted to main features. Tickets go on sale at the door about half an hour before show time.

It's 5:00 A.M.; you've been up most of the night watching for shooting stars and are famished. Head on over to the

Toms River Diner on Route 31, (732) 929–0440—it's open twenty-four hours a day.

The ***Popcorn Park Zoo*** in Forked River is the only institution of its kind in the United States. Popcorn Park was founded in 1977 by the Associated Humane Societies for the express purpose of taking in wild animals no longer able to fend for themselves due to age, infirmity, injury, or abuse by humans. Within a few years, however, the zoo's managers realized that their mission should be extended to domestic and exotic animals in distress, and so it was. Today's Popcorn Park Zoo is the home of last resort for all manner of creatures, from abandoned Easter chicks and rabbits to lions, tigers, mountain lions, bears—even an elephant—that were confined and abused by the shady operators of roadside animal shows and fly-by-night "circuses." All the creatures at Popcorn Park have one

Newarkies and Rah-Rahs

A long the boardwalks of the Jersey Shore in the 1960s, you could tell who was who by the clothes they wore. Among teenagers, there were two basic casts of characters: the Newarkies and the Rah-rahs. The Newarkies mostly came from the cities of North Jersey (hence the name), while the Rah-rahs were suburban kids. Newarkies hit the boardwalk wearing tight black pants, black shoes, and strap T-shirts. Rah-rahs wore white denim cutoffs, anything they could find that was made of madras, and sandals or—on formal occasions—penny loafers with no socks. They also surfed, or pretended they did. Newarkies, as well as we can recall, just hung out.

thing in common: They very likely would have not made it were it not for the zoo's open-door policy and expert care and for the kindness of those who brought them to this unique facility. What would have become of Marlboro, the goat, left for dead after a bizarre cult ritual; of Hawkeye, the rhesus monkey, found loose at Newark Airport after escaping from a contingent of monkeys bound for a research lab; or Rowdy, the three-legged raccoon?

Popcorn Park Zoo offers spacious, clean accommodations for its animals, and tamer species are allowed to wander freely on the grounds as much as possible. The zoo is situated on the eastern fringes of the New Jersey Pine Barrens, and landscaping is deliberately minimal—a natural scrub-forest environment prevails.

Popcorn Park Zoo, Humane Way at Lacey Road, Forked River 08731, (609) 693–1900, is open Monday through Friday, 1:00–5:00 P.M. during winter months; and daily 11:00 A.M.–5:00 P.M. during summer. Admission is $3.25 for adults; $2.25 for children and senior citizens.

Forked River is home to another classic Jersey diner—the *Forked River Diner* on Route 9. It's open daily 5:00 A.M.–3:00 P.M., except Christmas Day.

More than thirty years ago, a handful of musicians began to gather every Saturday night in the secluded deer camp of Joe and George Albert in the Waretown pinelands to play music. Known as the "Home Place," it became known as *the* place to go to hear down-home music. The "pickin' pineys" have changed venue several times over the years, but the "Sounds of the Jersey Pines" still ring out every Saturday night, and the pinelands musical heritage lives on.

Miniature Golf Tournament

*E*very summer Thursday morning at 9:30 sharp, dozens of the Jersey Shore's fiercest golf competitors gather at Bill Burr's Flamingo Golf, on the Boulevard in Ship Bottom. A tradition "for at least ten years," according to one volunteer scorekeeper, Burr's weekly miniature golf tournaments draw kids and adults alike. It's a microcosm of the Masters, with a slew of goofy obstacles that put Augusta National's ponds, bunkers, and azaleas to shame.

The Flamingo is serious about its little tournament: The summer's winners to date are always posted on a board near the entrance. The players are no less devoted, talking about their birdies and eagles and critical putts, and even dropping the occasional remark about their prowess on the full-size links . . . which is where you won't find them on Thursday morning.

In 1997 the Pineland Cultural Society, formed around the original members, completed construction of a new 6,000-square-foot building. The air-conditioned, 350-seat **Albert Music Hall** is now the site of year-round Saturday night concerts featuring country, bluegrass, and folk music.

The Albert Music Hall is at 125 Wells Mill Road (Route 532), Waretown 08758. Doors open at 7:00 P.M.; concerts begin at 8:00 P.M. and end at 11:30 P.M. Admission is $4.00 for adults and $1.00 for children under twelve. For more information contact the Pinelands Cultural Society, P.O. Box 657, Waretown 08758, (609) 971–1593.

Have a yen for some coconut-cluster toasted marshmallow? Milk pecan patties? Double-dipped chocolate mints? **Stutz Own Make Candies** has been making a wide variety of candies for almost sixty years. Their 2,000-square-foot factory at Fourteenth Street and Long Beach Boulevard, Ship Bottom, (609) 494–5303, is open year-round, off-season 10:00 A.M.–6:00 P.M. daily; in-season, 9:00 A.M.–10:30 P.M. daily. (Don't miss the cherry vanilla fudge!) Note: While Stutz candy is very sweet, the counter help can be quite sour.

Not too many tours include a stop to collect trash. But the folks that conduct the *ALO (Alliance for a Living Ocean) ECO-Tour of Long Beach Island* make the chore a pleasure—as they do with learning about the estuarine environment and how to protect and restore it. The trolley tour covers both ends of the island, giving riders "hands-on" environment lessons at various points en route. Among the stops: Barnegat Light, Edith Duff Gwynn Gardens, Viking Village, Brant Beach, Holgate (where stone lawns are sprayed with herbicides and pesticides that run off into local waters), and Beach Haven.

Red Flag's Up—Ladies Off the Beach!

Surf City, on Long Beach Island, was one of the first New Jersey Shore communities to feature resort hotels. At the "Mansion of Health," which flourished as early as the 1820s, men and women guests were assigned separate bathing times on the hotel's beachfront. A red flag was the signal for men to use the beach, and a white flag meant it was the ladies' turn. The system was vital for maintaining propriety and decorum— in those days, men swam nude at the Jersey Shore.

For tour information contact ALO at P.O. Box 95, Ship Bottom 08008, (609) 492–3896. Tours begin at 8:30 A.M. and cost $10 per person. Children five and under are free.

You can't drop in at the ***Green Gables Inn & Restaurant*** in Beach Haven on Long Beach Island, because dinner is by reservation only (call before 3:00 P.M.), and the inn is usually booked in advance. Nevertheless, if you're looking for a marvelous place to get away, this 1880s Victorian B&B/restaurant is worth planning ahead for.

The restaurant serves a $59-per-person, five-course candlelight dinner, whose components change weekly. A sampling: first course—seafood bisque, surrounded by fried spinach, puff-pastry cutouts, and calamari; second course—Portobello mushrooms, stuffed with prosciutto and Gruyère, sautéed, and served on a bed of greens vinaigrette; third course—artichokes in pasta-crepe bundles, tied with chives, and served in a puddle of light tomato sauce; fourth course—baked tuna and flounder, served on a bed of chopped spinach and herbs and topped with tomatoes, spiked with oregano; and, for dessert, a poached pear, wrapped in phyllo dough and served hot on a pool of caramel sauce, garnished with slices of strawberries and mint leaves.

If you're spending the night in one of the six guest rooms at the inn, which is listed in the National Register of Historic Places, do try to fit in a walk on the beach before the home-baked breakfast buffet.

Green Gables Inn & Restaurant, 212 Centre Street, Beach Haven, Long Beach Island 08008, (609) 492–3553, is open year-round. Dinner is served nightly, with seatings at 6:00 and 8:30 P.M. Reservations are a must.

One more lighthouse: This one is **Barnegat Light,** in **Barnegat Lighthouse State Park,** on the southern shore of Barnegat Inlet. "Old Barney," as shore residents call their now-extinguished beacon, was built in 1858 to replace an 1834 lighthouse that toppled during a flood. This time the government didn't fool around: Project engineer Gen. George Gordon Meade later famous as the Union Commander at Gettysburg, supervised the construction of a 168-foot tower, with brick walls that are 10 feet thick at the bottom and taper to an 18-inch thickness at the top. The illumination source was a five-ton Fresnel-lens monster, rotated smoothly on a bed of bronze rollers by a mechanism that resembled the innards of a giant grandfather clock. Every four minutes the beacon rotated, and lives and shipping were saved from the sands of Barnegat Beach.

Barnegat Light came to the end of its usefulness even earlier than Twin Lights at Navesink. The great structure was replaced by a lightship anchored offshore in 1927, but its dismantling was prevented by public sentiment and, probably, the fact that nothing short of a full-scale naval bombardment could have taken it down. So it survives as the focal point of a lovely state park that offers some of the Jersey Shore's best swimming, surf casting, and birding, not to mention sightseeing. Anyone who cares to mount the lighthouse's 217 steps, when the building is open, will be rewarded by a panoramic view of Barnegat Bay, the barrier beaches and the distant mainland, and the vast sweep of the Atlantic.

Barnegat Lighthouse State Park, Broadway, Barnegat Light 08006, (609) 494–2016, is open all year. The lighthouse is open weekends beginning May 1, daily

"Old Barney," a historic lighthouse, provides the focal point for Barnegat Lighthouse State Park, in Barnegat Light.

from June through the end of September, and weekends through October. It is also open some evenings in the summer. Call for specific times. There is a $1.00 fee for admission to the lighthouse.

Atlantic City Area

tar Route 72 is the only way on and off Long Beach Island, of which Barnegat Lighthouse State Park forms the northern tip. Right after you turn right at the town of Ship Bottom and head back toward the mainland on Route 72, you'll pass the Barnegat Division of the *Edwin B. Forsythe National Wildlife Refuge.* The crowning achievement in the struggle to keep the wetlands of the Jersey Shore from yielding entirely to development as well as a vital link in the fragile chain of stopover areas in the Atlantic flyway used by migratory birds, the refuge offers a refreshingly different coastal experience for human visitors, too. Although there are at this time no developed facilities for visitor use at the smaller Barnegat Division of the 40,000-acre refuge, the Brigantine Division, just across Reeds and Absecon Bays from Atlantic City, has a fine 8-mile auto-tour route and two short interpretive nature trails.

If you'd like to take the self-guided auto tour of the Brigantine Division of the refuge, plan on spending about an hour and a half. The tour begins at the division headquarters on Great Creek Road, off Route 9 at Oceanville, and makes a loop back to the starting point. Be sure to pick up a checklist of the refuge's bird species (more than 200 have been identified) at headquarters.

Headquarters of the Brigantine Division of the Edwin B. Forsythe National Wildlife Refuge is P.O. Box 72, Oceanville 08231 (for location, see above), (609) 652–1665. The refuge, auto route, and nature trails are open daily, all year, from sunrise to sunset. Admission is $4.00 per noncommercial vehicle.

By the Sea

*N*ew Jersey's 127 miles of white sandy beaches offer some of the finest swimming in the East. And like much of the state, they're a study in contrasts, ranging from the crowded, carnival atmosphere at Wildwood to the laid-back, genteel scene along the strand at Cape May. The prize for the most surreal bathing experience has to go to the beach at Atlantic City. The people who bustle along the boardwalk from one high-rise casino to another seem to exist in another dimension from that of the bathers romping on the uncrowded beaches just a few feet away.

Located in the midst of the wildlife refuge in the town of Tuckerton is one of New Jersey's newest museums, **Barnegat Bay Decoy and Baymen's Museum.** Opened in 1993, the museum is dedicated to preserving the heritage and culture of the Jersey Shore baymen.

More than 3,000 photographs chronicle the Barnegat Bay area's culture. Boat building, clamming, oystering, gunning, fishing, lifesaving, and charter boat operating are all well documented. A collection of traditionally built cedar boats includes the Barnegat Bay Sneakbox, the Jersey working garvey, and the Jersey skiff. Hand-carved wildfowl decoys, formerly utilitarian objects, are now relics of American folk art and a major display. The museum periodically features carvers such as Harry V. Shourds, who for forty years carved up to 2,000 decoys a year. Eeling baskets and a large assortment of tools and relics round out the collection.

The museum is re-creating an authentic working Tuckerton Seaport Village on a 40-acre waterfront site that will contain twenty-six existing historical struc-

A Very Long Wire

*T*he western terminus of the world's first fiber optic transatlantic cable is in Tuckerton.

tures and replicas of actual buildings from up and down Barnegat Bay, representing various traditional trades and crafts unique to the baymen of the Jersey Shore. Phase I, which will include eleven buildings (including the Decoy and Baymen's Museum) is scheduled for completion in the spring of 1999.

Barnegat Bay Decoy and Baymen's Museum, Route 9 at Tip Seaman Park, Tuckerton 08087, (609) 296–8868, is open Wednesday through Sunday 10:00 A.M.–4:30 P.M. Admission is $2.00 for adults, free for children under twelve.

Adjacent to the Forsythe National Wildlife Refuge, overlooking Lily Lake, is the *Noyes Museum of Art,* which features a collection of nineteenth- and twentieth-century American folk art from the Mid-Atlantic region. The Noyes Museum is the result of the interest, vision, and resources of two individuals—Fred W. Noyes, Jr., and his late wife, Ethel Marie. Mr. and Mrs. Noyes, antiques dealers and developers of the nearby Historic Towne of Smithville restoration, became interested during the mid-1970s in establishing a museum of American arts and crafts.

Approximately 200 North American decoys are a major exhibit at the museum. The carving of decoys, at one time an indigenous cottage industry on the Jersey Shore, is

North American decoys are on display at the Noyes Museum of Art.

now recognized as an important branch of folk art. In addition to the Noyes decoy collection, the museum exhibits its collection of contemporary American art and crafts and mounts twelve to fifteen exhibitions annually. It also features special exhibitions of works by leading regional artists. Special "Meet the Artist" days are

Improving the Plovers' Odds

*W*ithin sight of the casino towers of Atlantic City, there are low, sandy wilderness islands that hardly anyone ever visits. Some, in fact, are absolutely off limits—they're managed as part of the Edwin B. Forsythe National Wildlife Refuge as breeding grounds for endangered bird species, most notably the piping plover. Plovers nest on the ground, where their eggs and newly hatched chicks are in danger not only from human intrusion, but from the predations of foxes, raccoons, and other creatures of the barrier beach islands. Refuge personnel erect mesh enclosures over the plovers' nests, designed to allow the parent birds and their chicks access, while keeping predators out.

We visited one such island, with a government biologist as our guide, and can report that the plovers have on their side a far better deterrent to unauthorized human visitors than mere warning signs. In the summer, the biting greenhead flies are so thick on these islands that our pens began to melt from the volume of repellent we were forced to use.

scheduled to coincide with the special exhibitions.

The Noyes Museum, Lily Lake Road, Oceanville 08231, (609) 652–8848, is open Wednesday through Sunday 11:00 A.M.–4:00 P.M. Admission is $3.00 for adults, $2.00 for senior citizens, 50 cents for full-time students, and free for children ages five through eighteen. Admission is free to all every Friday.

You have to go through Atlantic City to get to the Marine Mammal Stranding Center in Brigantine (see directions below), and, from there it's only a 1-block detour to the **White House Sub Shop** at 2301 Arctic Avenue, (609)

345–8599. The "Home of Submarines" is hardly undiscovered: Their sign advertises OVER 15 MILLION SOLD and the restaurant is a favorite stop for visiting celebrities. The sandwiches are huge and delicious (unless you're positively ravenous, share one or buy a half). The shop is open Monday through Saturday 10:00 A.M.–midnight, and Sunday 11:00 A.M.–midnight.

After you've eaten, follow signs for Trump Castle Casino and State Marina to the Brigantine Bridge (between Harrah's and Trump Castle) into Brigantine. The *Marine Mammal Stranding Center and Sea Life Museum* is on the left, 2 miles past the bridge. Since its founding in 1978, this private, nonprofit center has responded to more than 1,000 calls about stranded whales, dolphins, seals, and sea turtles that washed ashore on New Jersey beaches. The animals are brought to the center for rehabilitation and eventual release.

The museum offers visitors a glimpse into New Jersey's undersea world. Displays and an aquarium focus on local marine life. At the center there are observation and closed-circuit television areas, where visitors can watch marine mammals exercising or receiving treatment. The center also conducts dolphin-watching cruises, where groups can see wildlife in natural surroundings and learn about the local/regional ecosystem.

The Marine Mammal Stranding Center and Sea Life Museum is in Brigantine (mailing address: P.O. Box 773, Brigantine 08203), (609) 266–0538. It is open daily 11:00 A.M.–5:00 P.M., Memorial Day to Labor Day; open weekends noon–4:00 P.M., the day after Labor Day to Memorial Day. Donations are welcome.

One of the Jersey Shore's greatest pieces of folk art—and far and away the largest—stands just south of Atlantic City at Margate City. She's **Lucy the Elephant,** a ninety-ton folly, left over from the great age of American looniness.

At one time giant walk-in animals and other outsized curiosities were not at all uncommon on America's roadways. Especially after the automobile caught on, entrepreneurs just naturally assumed that travelers would want to stop for coffee in a shop shaped like a coffeepot or buy a dressed duck for dinner from a vendor in a huge cement duck (we kid you not—just such a monster fowl was saved not long ago by preservationists on Long Island). James V. Lafferty wasn't selling elephants when, in 1881, he built Lucy on the sands of South Beach in what was then South Atlantic City; he was trying to develop a resort. Since he couldn't use free VCRs as a come-on in those days, he decided to construct an elephant that everyone would want to come and see.

Lucy is a six-story wonder. Made out of sheet metal over a wooden frame, she has 20-foot-long legs, a 38-foot-long body, and a covered howdah on her back to serve as an observation deck. Inside were spiral staircases (they ran up Lucy's hind legs) and a restaurant. If having lunch in the belly of an elephant didn't make you want to buy one of Lafferty's house lots, well, you were just against progress.

Lafferty sold Lucy in 1887 to local hoteliers Sophie and John Gertzen. They made her the namesake and an annex of their Elephant Hotel, and even after the hotel closed and John Gertzen passed away, his widow kept

Atlantic City Facts

*D*id you know that in Atlantic City . . .

The year-round population numbers fewer than 38,000, but more than 30 million people visit each year.

When the first casino opened in 1978, the line of people waiting to get in wrapped all the way around the building.

The twelve casinos contain 21,186 slot machines.

Saltwater taffy got its name after a candy store on the boardwalk was flooded during a storm.

The first boardwalk was built in 1870, to keep sand out of ladies' shoes.

the elephant open. Unfortunately, by the time Mrs. Gertzen died in 1963, Lucy was creaky in her bones and shabby in her outward appearance, and officials with no sense of humor had her condemned.

Just in the nick of time, Lucy was saved by—what else?—a Save Lucy Committee. The state declared her a historic site, and a movable site at that. In 1970 she was transported to her present location.

Lucy the Elephant stands on the beach at the head of Decatur Avenue in Margate City. She is open daily, 10:00 A.M.–8:00 P.M., mid-June through Labor Day; on weekends only, 10:00 A.M.–4:30 P.M., mid-April through mid-June and from Labor Day through October; closed in winter. A tour of Lucy begins with a ten-minute video on her history, continues with a guided tour through various rooms filled with artifacts and photographs, and ends at the top in Lucy's howdah, which affords a fabulous ocean view. Admission is $2.00 for adults, $1.00 for children twelve and under. Call (609) 823–6473 for more information.

Art lovers won't want to miss **Roslyn Sailor Fine Arts,** said to be the largest private gallery in the world. The gallery exhibits the works of thirty-five to forty contemporary artists at a time and has an extensive art library. The gallery, at 8401 Ventnor Avenue, Margate 08402, (609) 822–2446, is open daily in summer, 11:00 A.M.–5:00 P.M., and Sunday, noon–5:00 P.M.; call for off-season hours.

Back on the mainland in Somers Point is the oldest house in all Atlantic County, the **Somers Mansion.** The three-story brick home was built between 1720 and 1726 by Richard Somers, scion of one of the first families to settle at the mouth of the Great Egg Harbor River. The house remained in the hands of the Somers family until 1937, when it was given to the Atlantic County Historical Society.

Now the property of the State of New Jersey, the Somers Mansion has been carefully refurnished with eigh-teenth-century antiques to suggest its character and appearance at the time Richard Somers made it his home. Accessories, acquired over the years by the Atlantic County Historical Society, include paintings, chinaware, quilts, and samplers. The overall effect is significantly different from that encountered in most northeastern colonial restorations, which are often based upon the lives and habitations of people of very modest means; here, on the south shore of New Jersey, we begin to find the northern fringes of the plantation style. Indeed, the 3,000-acre Somers property was called Somerset Plantation . . . and Somers Point is a lot closer to Virginia than it is to Massachusetts.

The Somers Mansion, Shore Road, Somers Point 08244, (609) 927–2212, is open Friday and Saturday 10:00 A.M.–noon and 1:00–4:00 P.M. and Sunday 1:00–4:00 P.M. Admission is free.

We can't pass Ocean City without visiting a reminder of what happened when lighthouse sentinels weren't properly heeded. Here is the **Ocean City Historical Museum** and its roomful of exhibits concerning the wreck of the *Sindia* on December 15, 1901. The *Sindia* was a four-masted barque on the last leg of her voyage from Japan to New York. Pressing northward along the Jersey coast in the teeth of a northeasterly gale, with her officers snug in their quarters and sure that nothing was going to go wrong this close to home, the ship was at the mercy of inexperienced crewmen, keeping watch above decks. Seeing a light off to port and assuming it was Sandy Hook, the helmsman rammed *Sindia* onto the bar off Ocean City. There she remains to this day, buried beneath the sand. The museum's Sindia Room tells the history of this famous wreck, with photographs, videos, charts, and articles—either retrieved from the wreck or washed up on shore—that include many beautiful pieces of Oriental pottery that never made it to the holiday tables of 1901 New York. Other rooms in the museum chronicle the landsman's life of early Ocean County. The domestic atmosphere of the era of Ocean City's 1879 founding is suggested in a series of authentically decorated Victorian rooms, complete with mannequins dressed in period costumes.

The museum's Historical Home, at 1139 Wesley Avenue, features an authentic seashore "cottage" built in 1919. It's open June 1–Labor Day (call 609–399–1801 for hours).

The Ocean City Historical Museum, 1735 Simpson Avenue, Ocean City 08226, (609) 339–1801, is open in summer, Monday through Friday 10:00 A.M.–4:00 P.M., and Saturday 1:00–4:00 P.M.; in winter, Tuesday through Saturday 1:00–4:00 P.M. (winter hours subject to change). Donations are appreciated.

Shriver's, the oldest continuously operating business on Ocean City's boardwalk, has been making saltwater taffy since 1898. The shop, on Ninth Street, (609) 399–0100, also makes great fudge.

If your beachcombing has left you empty-handed, stop at the *Discovery Seashell Museum and Shell Yard.* The museum, which exhibits and sells shells and corals from around the world, is at 2721 Asbury Avenue, Ocean City, (609) 398–2316; open Memorial Day through September 9:00 A.M. to 8:00 P.M., and 10:00 A.M. to 5:00 P.M. the rest of the year. There is no admission fee.

Cape May

C ape May's *Stone Harbor Bird Sanctuary* is far, far smaller than the vast tracts protected by the federal government at the Brigantine and Barnegat sites, but it is no less vital to a major group of avian species. Stone Harbor is a heronry, the only one in the United States that is municipally sponsored. It's the nesting place of numerous species of the heron family, including American egret, snowy egret, Louisiana heron, green heron, black-crowned night heron, yellow-crowned night heron, and even the more recently arrived cattle egret. Another recent arrival, having shown up for the first time in 1958, is the glossy ibis. These dark-bronze birds, with their long, slender, downturned bills, are the only nesting species at Stone Harbor that are not members of the heron family.

The best time for birders to come to the Stone Harbor Sanctuary is between March and October. The herons, egrets, and ibis build nests and raise their young in spring; later in the season, in the final months prior to their southward migrations, the birds keep to a schedule that takes them almost en masse from their nesting areas in the sanctuary to feeding grounds in the marshes at dawn and back again to the sanctuary at dusk. Often ungainly on their stiltlike legs, herons and their kin are creatures of remarkable grace when they take wing, and to see them in such numbers at first and last light is a rare treat.

Stone Harbor Bird Sanctuary, located between Second and Third Avenues and 111th and 116th Streets, Stone Harbor 08247, (609) 368–5102, is open all year. Visitors are restricted to the observation area adjacent to the parking lot on Third Avenue, where there are a species identification chart and coin-operated binoculars. There is no charge for parking.

Another Stone Harbor "must see" is *The Wetlands Institute,* an organization dedicated to scientific research and public education concerning intertidal salt marshes and other coastal systems. Begun in 1969 by conservationist Herbert H. Mills, the institute's facilities include a main building, housing exhibits and lecture halls; a gift shop; a library; salt-marsh and aquatic exhibits, with touch tank and touch tables with microscopes; and interactive exhibits for children. There's also a tower that offers a bird's-eye view of the surrounding salt marsh. Outdoors are a salt marsh trail, a boardwalk, and a 100-foot pier over a tidal creek. The surrounding salt marsh is part of a 6,000-acre publicly owned tract of coastal wetlands.

The Wetlands Institute, 1075 Stone Harbor Boulevard, Stone Harbor 08247, (609) 368–1211, is open year-round: from May 15 through October 15, Monday through Saturday 9:30 A.M.–4:30 P.M., and Sunday 10:00 A.M.–4:00 P.M.; from October 15 through May 15, closed Sunday and Monday. Admission is $5.00 for adults, $2.00 for children.

If we were to have to pick the most tranquil and inspiring spot in Cape May County, Stone Harbor Bird Sanctuary might well be tied with **Leaming's Run Gardens and Colonial Farm** in nearby Swainton. Leaming's Run (it's named after a brook that flows through the property, which in turn is named after a whaler and early settler of Cape May) makes better horticultural use out of a scant twenty acres than any similar place we've seen. At Leaming's Run a mile-long path leads to twenty-seven individual annual gardens, each with its own theme and color scheme.

Between mid-June and early October, there is always something in bloom at Leaming's Run. August is an especially enchanting time, as the gardens attract thousands of hummingbirds—Leaming's Run has, in fact, become known as the "Hummingbird Capital of the East." Given the garden's spectacular palette of colors and the pervasive smell of honeysuckle, it isn't hard to understand the attraction they hold for the tiny, hovering birds.

A special attraction at Leaming's Run is the Colonial Farm, a small compound of log buildings that faithfully replicates a pioneer homestead of Cape May County circa 1695. Every detail of the tiny cabin, with its chimney of mud and logs, is true to the days when Cape May men like Thomas Leaming went whaling while their families waited and kept busy on farms like these.

Leaming's Run Gardens and Colonial Farm, Route 9, Swainton (Cape May Court House) 08210, (609) 465–5871, is open daily 9:30 A.M.–5:00 P.M. May 15 through October 20. The Cooperage gift shop is open daily 10:00 A.M.–5:00 P.M. Admission to the gardens and farm is $4.50 for adults, $1.00 for children ages six through twelve. Annual tickets, available for $10.00 per person, allow unlimited visits throughout the season.

If you don't think a stay at the **_Candlelight Inn_** is worth dying for, choose to stay at a time they're not hosting one of their Murder by Candlelight weekends. The inn, a beautifully restored turn-of-the-century Queen Anne Victorian, is decorated to a fare-thee-well with antiques, Oriental rugs, and old prints. All rooms have private baths; some have air-conditioning, and others, ceiling fans. Suites in the renovated carriage house are air-conditioned and have fireplaces, Jacuzzis, and a wet bar.

Guests are invited to sip sherry on the spacious, wraparound veranda or soak in the hot tub on the outdoor sundeck (a truly wonderful experience on a moonlit night). A full breakfast, included in the rate, is served on antique dishes in the elegantly appointed, nineteenth-century dining room. Prices range from $85 to $260—the top tarriff gets you a two-bedroom, two-bath suite. The inn is on the shore at 2310 Central Avenue, North Wildwood 08260, (609) 522–6200.

Groff's in Wildwood has been serving families moderately priced meals since 1925, and the food is great. The Groff family prides itself on its desserts; among house specialties are black-bottom pie, blueberry glaze, lemon meringue, and coconut cream pie. The restaurant, at Magnolia and Boardwalk, (609) 522–5474, is open daily, 4:00–8:00 P.M. Take-out is available.

Wyland Whaling Wall #43, the work of international environmental muralist Wyland, is at Garfield Avenue and the Boardwalk in Wildwood.

Another Cape May Court House site worth visiting is the *Cape May County Historical and Genealogical Society Museum*. The history of Cape May County is a bit different from that of the rest of the New Jersey shore; nearly 300 years ago this was whaling country, and many of the old Cape May families were emigrants from New England. (One of the attractions of the museum's library to geneologists, in fact, is its wealth of material that chronicles the Mayflower connections of many of the county's early inhabitants.)

The museum is quartered in the John Holmes House, which, like many very old eastern seaboard homes, is an amalgamation of structures erected at different times. The oldest section is the rear portion, believed to have been built in the mid-1700s and at one time the center of an estate that totaled nearly 400 acres. What is now the main section of the house was added just before 1800 by John Holmes, an Irish immigrant to Cape May County.

The collections of the museum generally relate to the working life of rural Cape May in the eighteenth and nineteenth centuries. In the adjacent barn are exhibits of whaling equipment, decoys, and maritime artifacts (including the lighthouse lens that formerly stood atop the tower at Cape May Point). In the museum proper are period rooms that illustrate colonial through Victorian living arrangements, a collection of early glassware, and assorted furnishings and chinaware. Most interesting, as long as you don't let your imagination wander, is the collection of surgical instruments in the medical room. These particularly relate to military medicine, and they document field surgical practices from the Revolution to the Spanish-American War. We gather that in the eighteenth century, what you did was pray for a clean hit to take you away all at once rather than leave you for the doctors to work on—a clean hit, say, from a musket such as those displayed in an adjacent room along with swords, uniforms, and other military paraphernalia, covering America's wars from the Revolution to Vietnam.

The Cape May County Historical Genealogical Society Museum, 504 Route 9, Cape May Court House 08210, (609) 465-3535, is open year-round, Tuesday through Saturday 8:30 A.M.–4:30 P.M. Self-guided tours are available daily 9:00 A.M.–4:00 P.M. (with the last ticket sold at 3:15). Donation is $2.50 for adults, 50 cents for children under twelve, and free for children under six. Guided tours, lasting approximately 1½ hours, are given daily at 10:30 A.M. and 2:00 P.M. Donation for these are $4.50 for adults, $1.00 for children under twelve, and free for children under six. The museum is available to visitors on Saturdays throughout the winter. The Genealogical Library is open Wednesday–Friday 9:00 A.M.–4: 00 P.M. year-round.

The *Cape May County Zoo* is one of the Jersey Shore's biggest surprises. Perhaps it's because when we think of the shore we think of sea creatures, not landlubbers like giraffes, lions, or camels. Nor do we expect to find an African savanna where sable antelopes, kudus, zebras, buffalo, ostriches, and elk roam freely.

There are nearly 250 species of animals, birds, and reptiles on 128 wooded acres here, including a reptile house with four large alligators. Feeding times are Tuesday and Friday at 2:00 P.M.

The Cape May County Zoo, Route 9 and Crest Haven Road, Cape May Court House 08210, (609) 465–5271, is open daily from 10:00 A.M. to 4:45 P.M. Admission is free, but donations are most welcome.

The town of *Cape May,* at the very tip of Cape May, is the sort of place that doesn't *have* attractions; it *is* one. Much of the "city" is a perfect period piece, a throwback to the days when a middle- or upper-middle-class vacation meant a long stay in a big hotel somewhere where the air was supposed to be good for you, and not two weeks in a car or tour bus. Cape May's career as a popular resort began very modestly just after 1800, when the only way to get here was by boat. By 1875 or so, at which time places like Atlantic City and Newport were just getting started, Cape May was a comfortable and thriving resort that could boast of having played host to presidents Pierce, Buchanan, Lincoln, and Grant. Its whaling days might be over, but its newfound gentility and taste were sure to carry it through the next century as a place to see and be seen.

Well, not quite. Cape May City did fade as the twentieth century matured; thirty years ago, few summer vacationers or beach-weekenders ventured south of the neon-lit motels of Wildwood unless they were of a certain age. Then Cape May began to benefit from the desire of more and more travelers to get away from their kind and from the revival of interest in Victorian architecture. Cape May had plenty of that particular commodity, despite its notorious combustibility— private homes, hotels, cottages, and guest houses, festooned with gingerbread aplenty, had survived quite nicely into the neon-motel era, needing only paint and patrons. Cape May has gotten to be fashionable once again, even if we haven't seen any presidents rocking on the porches of late.

Today the "Nation's Oldest Seashore Resort" is a National Historic Landmark Site, with more than 600 authentically restored and preserved Victorian structures.

Perhaps the most impressive of Cape May's Victorian mansions is the ***Emlen Physick Estate,*** designed by the eminent Philadelphia architect Frank Furness and built in 1879. The Physick Estate belongs to that school of mid-to-late-Victorian architecture called the Stick Style, in which the structural features of a building were made apparent through the use of exposed exterior timbers. The result was something of a framework effect, elaborated upon by means of steep-gabled, overhanging roof planes, hooded dormers, and a broad veranda, supported by arches almost Gothic in character. A Furness signature, and a staple on finely detailed houses of the related Queen Anne and Shingle styles as well, was the use of massive, heavily ornamented chimneys—quite an ambitious approach for a beach cottage, all in all.

Tours of the Physick Estate can be arranged through the Mid-Atlantic Center for the Arts, an umbrella group that is deeply involved in local preservation and cultural affairs. The center offers a number of interesting tour packages and separate events, including an evening "gaslight" tour of select-ed mansions of the Victorian era; interior tours of selected houses, combined with afternoon tea; historic-district walking tours of Cape May City; and special children's tours. The center sponsors theater, a Victorian Week in October, and a full schedule of Christmas events.

The Mid-Atlantic Center for the Arts is headquartered at the Physick Estate, 1048 Washington Street (P.O.Box 340), Cape May 08204, (609) 884–5404. The tour of the Physick Estate costs $6.00 for adults, $3.00 for children; the Mansions by Gaslight tour cost is $10.00, and the Innteriors Tours and Teas are $12.00. Contact the center for further information.

The innkeepers at the Victorian *Mainstay Inn* describe their rooms and suites as ranging "from ostentatious Victorian splendor to contemporary elegance," and elegance indeed defines this magnificent Italianate villa

The Emlen Physick Estate remains an impressive example of Cape May's Victorian mansions.

built in 1872 as a gentlemen's gambling and entertainment club. Architectural highlights include 14-foot ceilings, elaborate chandeliers, a veranda, and a cupola.

The Mainstay Inn, 635 Columbia Avenue, Cape May 08204, (609) 884–8690, is open mid-March through New Year's Eve; the Officers' Quarters is open year-round. There is a three-night minimum stay in season. Rates range from $95 to $195. The nonsmoking inn (except on the veranda) is not appropriate for small children.

In 1850 a Philadelphia chemist named William Weightman built a summer home in the Second Empire style of architecture at the corner of Washington and Franklin Streets in Cape May. In 1884 his son wanted to be closer to the beach, so he bought property on Ocean Avenue, had the building cut in half, and got farmers with horses and logs to move the house. In 1962 the Reverend Carl McIntyre purchased the Weightman buildings to save them from demolition and moved them to their present site on Reading Avenue.

In February 1989 John and Barbara Girton purchased the deteriorating structures and put 53,000 hours of work and more than $3 million into restoring the property. In June 1989 they opened the fifty-seven-room, twenty-six-guest-room B&B *Angel of the Sea.* In 1990 this gingerbread Victorian placed second in the National Trust for Historic Preservation's Bed and Breakfast Inns contest and has since been selected by two national bed-and-breakfast organizations as one of the top ten in the country. This truly magnificent inn is at 5–7 Trenton Avenue, Cape May 08204, (609) 884–3369.

Each spring millions of horseshoe crabs come up the Delaware Bay to beaches near East Point Lighthouse at the mouth of the Maurice River to lay their eggs. And each year, at the same time, millions of shorebirds migrating north from South America arrive just in time to snack down on the eggs, refueling for the long flight still to come. Each year, from September to November, Cape May Point becomes the Raptor Capital of North America as an estimated 50,000 migrating hawks pass over.

To learn about these—and other—avian happenings on Cape May Peninsula, visit either of the *Cape May Bird Observatory*'s two locations: Audubon North Woods Center, Cape May Point, (609) 884–2736, open daily 9:00 A.M. to 5:00 P.M.; or the Center for Research and

Education, 600 Route 47N, Cape May Court House 08210, (609) 861–0700, open Tuesday through Sunday 9:00 A.M.–5:00 P.M. The Birding Hotline: (609) 861–0466.

The historic 1859 ***Cape May Lighthouse*** at the mouth of the Delaware Bay, one of the oldest continually operating lighthouses in the United States, is open to the public for tours. Now owned by the State of New Jersey, the lighthouse is undergoing extensive renovations under the watchful eye of the Mid-Atlantic Center for the Arts, Victorian Cape May's leader in historic preservation and the performing arts. Work has been completed on the Oil House, now a visitors' orientation center.

Cape May Lighthouse, Cape May Point State Park, Lighthouse Road, Cape May Point, (609) 884–5404, is open year-round: spring, fall, and winter 10:00 A.M.–4:00 P.M., and summer months 9:00 A.M.–6:00 P.M. Admission to the Oil House is free. Admission to the lighthouse tower is $3.50 for adults, allowing one child to climb free per adult. Additional children are admitted at $1.00 each.

The ***Cape May Shoreline Railroad*** is one of the area's newest attractions. Using the original equipment of an early rail company that operated in South Jersey, the train makes four round-trips daily between Cape May and Tuckahoe during the summer, and also operates weekends year-round, stopping at the Cape May County Park and Zoo, the Cape May Court House, and Historic Cold Spring Village. The train provides free shuttle service from the zoo. For schedules and fare information call (609) 898–2300.

Cape May Ferry, which traverses Delaware Bay

between Cape May and the picturesque town of Lewes, Delaware, is the most convenient way to travel from the Jersey Shore to Delmarva Peninsula resorts such as Rehoboth Beach, Delaware, and Ocean City, Maryland. It leaves from North Cape May and operates all year. Write Cape May Terminal, P.O. Box 827, North Cape May 08204, or call 1–800–64FERRY or (609) 886–9699 for a schedule and rates.

PLACES TO STAY
AT THE SHORE

ATLANTIC VIEW INN
20 Woodland Avenue, Avon-by-the-Sea 07717; (732) 774–8505; fax (732) 869–0187

BERKELEY CARTERET HOTEL
1401 Ocean Avenue, Asbury Park 07712; (888) 776–6701 or (732) 776–6700; fax (732) 776–9546

CANDLELIGHT INN
2310 Central Avenue, North Wildwood 08260; (609) 522–6200

CARISBROOKE INN
105 South Little Rock Avenue, Ventnor 08406; (609) 822–6392; fax (609) 822–9710

THE CHATEAU
500 Warren Avenue, Spring Lake Beach 07762; (732) 974–2000; fax (732) 974–0007

CONOVER'S BAY HEAD INN
646 Main Avenue, Bay Head 08742; (800) 956–9099 or (732) 892–4664

GRAND HOTEL OF CAPE MAY
Ocean at Philadelphia Avenue, Box 496, Cape May 08204; (800) 257–8550 or (609) 884–5611; fax (609) 898–0341

THE HEWITT WELLINGTON
200 Monmouth Avenue, Spring Lake 07762; (732) 974–1212

LA MAISON
404 Jersey Avenue, Spring Lake 07762; (732) 449–0969

MARQUIS DE LAFAYETTE HOTEL
501 Beach Drive, Cape May 08204; (800) 257–0432 or (609) 884–0669

THE MASON COTTAGE
625 Columbia Avenue, Cape May 03204; (800) 716–2766 or (609) 884–3358

SEASCAPE MANOR
3 Grand Tour, Highlands 07732; (732) 291–8467; fax (732) 872–7932

PLACES TO EAT
AT THE SHORE

DUTCHMAN'S BRAUHAUS
2500 East Bay Avenue, Manahawkin, Cedar Bonnet Island; (609) 494–8909

EBBITT ROOM
(Virginia Hotel), 25 Jackson Street, Cape May;
(609) 884–5700

EUROPA SOUTH
521 Arnold Avenue, Point Pleasant Beach; (732) 295–1500
(Spanish/Portuguese cuisine)

410 BANK STREET
410 Bank Street, Cape May;
(609) 884–2127

JOE & MAGGIE'S BISTRO ON BROADWAY
591 Broadway, Long Branch;
(732) 571–8848

KUISHIMBO
322 Carpenter's Lane, Cape May;
(609) 884–0712
(Japanese cuisine)

LOBSTER HOUSE
Fisherman's Wharf, Cape May;
(609) 884–8296

THE MAD BATTER
Carroll Villa Hotel, 19 Jackson Street, Cape May;
(609) 884–5970

RAIMONDO'S
1101 Long Beach Boulevard, Ship Bottom; (609) 494–5391

TISHA'S FINE DINING
714 Beach Drive, Cape May;
(609) 884–9119

WATERFRONT CAFE
Navesink Marina, 1400 Ocean Avenue, Sea Bright;
(732) 741–2244

OTHER ATTRACTIONS
AT THE SHORE

ALGOR–BARKALOW HOMESTEAD MUSEUM
1701 New Bedford Road, Wall 07719; (732) 681–3806

ATLANTIC CITY BOARDWALK
Atlantic City

BARNEGAT LIGHT MUSEUM AND HISTORICAL SOCIETY
Fifth Street and Central Avenue, Barnegat 08006; (609) 494–8578

BEACH HAVEN GUIDED WALKING TOURS
Downtown Victorian district, Beach Haven 08008;
(609) 492–0700

CHURCH OF THE PRESIDENTS
1260 Ocean Avenue, Long Branch 07740; (732) 229–0600

HISTORIC COLD SPRING VILLAGE
720 Route 9, Cape May 08204;
(609) 898–2300

ISLAND BEACH STATE PARK
Route 35, Seaside Park 08752;
(732) 793–0506

JENKINSON'S AQUARIUM
Boardwalk and Parkway, Point Pleasant Beach 08742;
(732) 899–1212/899–1659

SPY HOUSE MUSEUM COMPLEX
119 Port Monmouth Road, Port Monmouth 07758; (732)
787–1807

ST. VLADIMIR'S MEMORIAL RUSSIAN ORTHODOX CHURCH
Rova Farms, 120 Cassville Road, Route 571, Jackson 08527;
(732) 928–1337/929–1248

U.S. ARMY COMMUNICATIONS ELECTRONICS MUSEUM
Off parkway exit 105, Building 275, Kaplan Hall, Fort Monmouth 07703; (732) 532–4390

WOODROW WILSON HALL
Monmouth University, Norwood and Cedar Avenues, West Long Branch 07764; (732) 571–3400

Selected Regional Information Centers, Chambers of Commerce, and Visitor Centers at the Shore

Atlantic City Convention and Visitors Authority, *2314 Pacific Avenue, Atlantic City 08401,*
(800) BOARDWK

Cape May County Department of Tourism and Economic Development,
P.O. Box 365, Cape May Court House 08210,
(609) 886–0901

Monmouth County Department of Promotion/Tourism,
6 West Main Street, Freehold 07728,
(800) 523–2587;
*Web site: **http://www.shore.co.monmouth.nj.us/-pubinfo***

Ocean County Public Affairs/Tourism,
101 Hooper Avenue, P.O. Box 2191, Toms River 08754,
(732) 929–2138 for information/questions; (800) ENJOY 33
for tourism guides

Ocean Grove Area Chamber of Commerce,
P.O. Box 415, Ocean Grove 07756, (732) 774–1391 (in New
Jersey); (800) 388–4768 (out-of-state)

Southern New Jersey

I n a small state like New Jersey, if there is any such thing as *terra incognita*—a part of the state that is least understood by the people in the other parts—then surely it is southern New Jersey, called South Jersey by New Jerseyans. South Jersey properly includes the Shore, but that's not what we're talking about here. The Shore is a land unto itself, and everybody thinks they know it, whether for the right or wrong reasons. But that vast bulge of land west of the littoral, tucked between Philadelphia and Delaware Bay, is what we're after.

South Jersey contains the least densely populated part of the nation's most densely populated state, the Pine Barrens, which even most Jerseyans hadn't heard of twenty years ago. The Pine Barrens are better known and even appreciated now, thanks in part to the environmentalists' crusade that brought much of their remote, scrubby acreage under strict state development guidelines and, in some areas, outright protection. At stake in the Barrens is not only a sense of wilderness so close to civilization but also a wonderfully pure water supply in a state that desperately needs it. The Pine Barrens' great water resource is not merely on the surface, in the still blue rivers and ponds that bring so many canoeists down this way, but in a vast underground aquifer, which could easily be poisoned or depleted by reckless development.

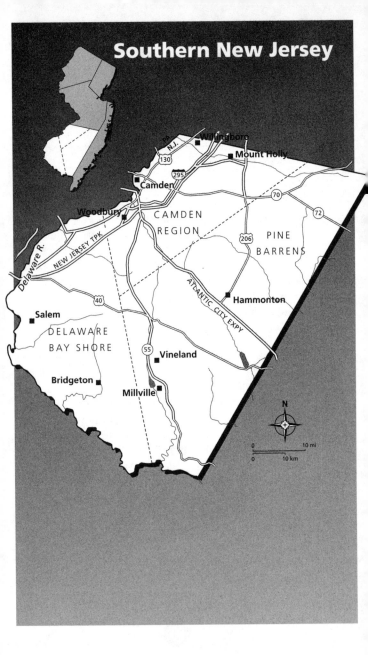

SOUTHERN NEW JERSEY'S TOP PICKS

Batsto

Bel Haven Canoe Rentals

Renault Winery

Wheaton Village

Vineland Produce Auction

A. J. Meerwald

Greenwich

Bridgeton Hall of Fame All Sports Museum

New Sweden Farmstead/Museum

Seabrook Educational and Cultural Center

Old Alloway Merchandise

Salem Court House

Finn's Point National Cemetery

Salem Oak

Cowtown Rodeo

Old Swedes Inn

Mullica Hill

C. A. Nothnagle Log House

Pomona Hall

Riverbus

Barclay Farmstead

Tandoor Palace

American Indian Heritage Museum

Elsewhere in South Jersey we find the big truck farms that produce those wonderful tomatoes for which New Jersey is justly famous—why else do you suppose the Campbell Soup Company is in Camden? Along the "other shore" of New Jersey, the coast of Salem and Cumberland Counties along Delaware Bay, are salt marshes and tidal estuaries, quilted with federal and state wildlife-management holdings. Here, at the mouths of meandering rivers like the Maurice and the Cohansey, are towns that seem as if they belong on the eastern shore of Maryland rather than in New Jersey, but the distance from Delaware Bay to the Chesapeake Bay isn't very far at all.

Finally as the bay narrows to a river and the river banks surrender their marshes to wharves and factories, we approach Camden and the great bridges to Philadelphia. Here southwestern New Jersey becomes very much like the northeastern part of the state, a dense cluster of towns and suburbs that would make a respectable metropolitan area anywhere else, but which are ever in the shadow of an urban goliath across the river.

Note: The orientation in this chapter is more or less counterclockwise, starting in the upper eastern corner of the region in the Pine Barrens, then heading down toward the Delaware Bay Shore, and finally going up the river to the Camden Region.

Pine Barrens

lsewhere in New Jersey, at Ringwood and at Allaire, we have come upon reminders of the days when iron mining, smelting, and forging were big industries in

Authors' Favorite Attractions in Southern New Jersey

A. J. Meerwald

American Indian Heritage Museum

Batsto

Finn's Point National Cemetery

Renault Winery

Seabrook Educational and Cultural Center

Wheaton Village

Top Annual Events in Southern New Jersey

Note: Schedules may vary; call ahead.

Apple Farm Arts and Music Festival, *Elmer; May;*
(609) 358–2472

Riverfest, *Red Bank; June; (732) 741–0055*

Delaware Bay Day, *East Point Light, Matt's Landing, Port Norris,*
Bivalve and Shellpile; June; (609) 785–2060

New Jersey State Fair, *Cherry Hill; July; (800) 749–3247*

Chatsworth Cranberry Festival, *Chatsworth, October;*
(609) 859–9701

Grand Christmas Exhibition, *Wheaton Village, Millville; late*
November/early January; (609) 825–6800

the state. The greatest of all New Jersey's old iron towns, however, is in the Pine Barrens, deep within the 110,000-acre **Wharton State Forest.** This is **Batsto,** which, in two centuries, has made the transition from busy industrial village to ghost town to major restoration.

Like the lands that surround Allaire Village, the environs of Batsto yield bog iron that can be collected on or near the surface. In 1766 Burlington attorney and provincial assemblyman Charles Read and a group of associates built a string of four ironworks in the bog-iron country of South Jersey, of which Batsto was to become the most famous. Little could he have known how famous, and how soon: Within ten years, under a later owner named John Cox, the furnace at Batsto was producing a steady stream of munitions for the Continental army. So important were the cannon and cannonballs cast at Batsto to the American war effort that the men who worked there were exempt from military service. This was a powerful inducement to owner Cox to keep the fires burning, as he was a Quaker pacifist who was initially disinclined to use his works for military production.

The British and their Tory allies were very much interested in what was going on at Batsto. Spies regularly reported on shipments of munitions from the works by wagon and by barge along the Mullica River, and on occasion, in 1778, a British detachment got as close to the forges as Chestnut Neck, near the mouth of the Mullica. Nevertheless the great furnace stayed lit, and it was able to make the transition from military to peacetime production (among Batsto's domestic and commercial products of the era are two firebacks, cast to George Washington's specifications and installed at Mount Vernon).

In 1784 Batsto's great era began when the property was acquired by William Richards, who made Batsto into more than just an ironworks in the forest. It became a self-contained village, with virtually everything its workers needed—store, residences, stables, sawmill, icehouse, and farm. Richards also built the structure that still dominates Batsto today, the stuccoed mansion.

Richards retired in 1809, but his son and grandson carried on. The furnace itself was rebuilt in 1829, and in 1846 the first Batsto glass factory was erected.

Although glassmaking at Batsto was profitable enough for a second glass factory to be built in 1848, the great iron furnace was shut down for good that year. The reason was the same as at Allaire: Pennsylvania coal was too cheap for New Jersey charcoal to compete. The furnace was dismantled in 1855. Twelve years later the glassworks went out of business, and in 1874 fire leveled half of Batsto village.

Batsto was purchased by Philadelphia industrialist Joseph Wharton in 1876. When his initial plan to dam the local streams and rivers and sell the water to Camden and Philadelphia failed, he built a sawmill and underground silo, enlarged the mansion and transformed its appearance to reflect the Italianate style of architecture, and cleared vast areas of land to cultivate crops, including cranberries. By the end of the nineteenth century, Batsto had been transformed into a "gentleman's farm."

After Wharton died in 1909, the State of New Jersey had a chance to buy his property for $1 million. State officials said yes, but the voters, feeling frugal, said no. Now the stage was set for the complete dereliction of the Batsto buildings. What nature was accomplishing slowly, the U.S. Air Force proposed to finish quickly in 1954, when plans were announced for a jet-support depot that would have done for the Pine Barrens what the Port Authority's jetport scheme almost did for the Great Swamp. The state opposed the Air Force proposal, as did environmentalists and those who wished to save what was left of Batsto village. This time New Jersey opened its purse: For $3 million, the entire tract was purchased. Thus was Wharton State Forest created. Restoration of the village began in 1958 and has continued ever since.

Batsto today offers visitors a look at what life in a nineteenth-century Pine Barrens village was like. All summer long interpreters can be found in the workers' houses and such key buildings as the mansion and the sawmill. The crafts of weaving and pottery making are also demonstrated. Across the Batsto River milldam from the village are the general store and 1852 post office (open in summer), the gristmill and barns, a visitors' center with interpretive exhibits and museum shop, and the Batsto Mansion itself.

Historic Batsto Village, off Route 542 in Hammonton 08037, (609) 561–3262, is open daily throughout the year. The visitors' center is open from 9:00 A.M. to 4:30 P.M.; the village grounds are open dawn to dusk. Interpretive programs are offered Wednesday through Sunday. The village is closed on major holidays. Fees for the mansion tour are $2.00 for persons ages twelve and up, $1.00 for children ages six to eleven, and free for children under six years of age. A parking fee is in effect weekends and holidays from Memorial Day through Labor Day.

Beyond the village spreads Wharton State Forest, with its splendid facilities for hiking, camping, canoeing, horseback riding, hunting, and fishing. Camping is permitted year-round—both at developed areas and at seven primitive sites. Nine cabins, with indoor toilets, showers, hot and cold water, and bunks, are available for

The Jersey Devil

*T*hey didn't just pull the name of New Jersey's hockey team out of thin air.

There is a "Jersey Devil," at least in persistent folklore. Described as having the head of a horse, the wings of a bat, and a dragonlike body, the creature has been the terror of the Pine Barrens for over 250 years. According to legend, a Mrs. Leeds, of Estellville (though there are variations in the woman's name and town), learned she was pregnant for the thirteenth time and swore that if she had to have another child, "Let it be the devil." She got her wish, giving birth to a monstrosity that let out a screech, then flew up the chimney and into legend.

Accused over the years of every crime from raiding chicken coops to souring milk to killing whole ponds full of fish with its poisonous breath, the monster at one time carried a reward on his head of $100,000, dead or alive. But no one has ever been able to catch him: The Jersey Devil is still out there, raising hell.

public use. For information on camping and other facilities in Wharton State Forest, call (609) 561–3252 or write R.D. 9, Hammonton 08037.

What better way to appreciate the wilderness of the Pine Barrens than by taking a backcountry canoe trip along Upper Toms River as it winds and twists through typical Pine Barrens foliage. There are numerous places to rent canoes and kayaks throughout the area; most will help you arrange your trip—whether for two hours or two weeks—and provide transportation. Just to mention a few: ***Mick's Canoe Rental, Inc.,*** in Chatsworth (mailing address: Box 45, Route 563, Jenkins 08019), (609) 726–1380; regular season, April 1 to November 1; by appointment November 1 through March 30. ***Pineland Canoes, Inc.,*** on Route 527, 4 miles north of Route 70 and 7 miles south of exit 21 off I–195 (mailing address: R.D. 2, Box 212, Jackson 08527) (732) 364–0389; rental season is from mid-April to the end of October; closed Monday and Tuesday.

There are few things on earth—or water—more relaxing than floating down a river in a tube. The river sets the pace and does the work; you just lie back and relax. ***Bel Haven Canoe Rentals,*** in addition to renting canoes, also rents one-person tubes and will launch you on a two- or four-hour float down the Wading or Batsto Rivers. Life jackets, tubes, and transportation to and from the river are provided. Bring your refreshments in soft packaging and a thermos; no cans or bottles are allowed. The operation is open daily from 8:00 A.M., May 15 through September 30. The last trip leaves at 2:00 P.M., and all are done by 5:00 P.M. The cost is $8.00 per person for fewer than ten people, $7.00 per person for more than ten people. There's a minimum charge of $24.00. Bel Haven is on Route 542, Green Bank 08215, (609) 965–2205 or (800) 445–0593.

Muddy Waters

*T*he next time you're paddling along the rivers of the Pine Barrens, note the dark, brownish color of the water. The soil in the Barrens is highly acidic, and iron and other organic contents leach out from it into the rivers and streams.

Estell Manor County Park, 3 miles south of Mays Landing on Route 50, is the site of the ruins of Estellville Glassworks, an early nineteenth-century glass factory. The ruins have interpretive signs, and visitors can get an idea of how glass was made from 1825 to 1877. The center has educational displays and a live animal exhibit. The 1,672-acre park is open daily dawn to dusk. The nature center is open weekdays 8:00 A.M. to 4:00 P.M., and weekends and holidays 11:00 A.M. to 3:00 P.M. Closed major holidays. Admission is free. Call (609) 645–5960 for information. The park is part of the Atlantic County Division of Parks and Recreation, 109 State Highway 50, Mays Landing 08330.

New Jersey never gets much press as a wine-producing state, but it isn't for lack of trying on the part of the *Renault Winery* in Egg Harbor City. Louis Renault came to southern New Jersey from Rheims, France, in 1864, and the winery—surrounded by acres of vineyards—has been in business ever since. It even operated round-the-clock during Prohibition, when the proprietors made a 44-proof "medicinal tonic" under special government license (Jersey folk always believed in the salubrious effects of a good tonic). Today Renault produces Chablis, Cabernet Sauvignon, Colombard, Riesling, May wine, and even champagne—the winery was, in fact, the largest American maker of champagne before California and New York took over the lead.

Renault offers an excellent guided tour, which covers wine making and storage, as well as a visit to the firm's museum of glassware and antique wine presses and other equipment, and finishes with a participatory visit to the tasting room.

The Great Paisley Boom

*L*ook on a map of South Jersey's Pine Barrens and you won't see a city named Paisley. But in the late 1880s, real-estate promoters touted the "magic city" of Paisley as a place where colleges would soon jostle against conservatories, where artists and authors would count doctors and composers among their neighbors, and where agriculture and manufacturing alike would boom. There were offices selling Paisley properties in several major cities—in all, 13,000 lots on 1,400 acres were on the market.

Some 3,000 eager buyers took the bait, at prices of around $375 per acre (the promoters had paid roughly a hundredth of that amount), and waited for construction to take off. Trouble was, just about all of them waited. By 1890 there were twelve modest buildings in Paisley—and that was the high point of its development. It's all still Pine Barrens.

The winery serves lunch daily, except Sunday, in its Garden Cafe. In the past champagne really was made in the "méthode Champenoise" room, where, at present, dinner is served; the booths are actually one-hundred-year-old oaken casks. Dinners include an appetizer, homemade soup, a pasta dish, a sorbet, salad, and a choice of six entrees such as chicken and lobster paillard or herb-crusted veal medallions—all accompanied, naturally, by wine samplings. Brunch is served every Sunday, 10:30 A.M.–2:30 P.M. Reservations are required for dinner.

Renault Winery, 72 North Bremen Avenue, Egg Harbor City 08215, (609) 965–2111, is open Monday through Saturday (except Thanksgiving, Christmas, New Year's

Day, and Easter) 10:00 A.M.–5:00 P.M., Sundays and holidays noon–5:00 P.M. The last tour leaves at 4:15 P.M. Admission is $2.00 for adults; for those under eighteen, free.

Legend has it that **Sweetwater Casino** was once *the* place to go to play high-stakes poker. Now it's the place to go to sit, have a drink and/or meal, and watch the Mullica River roll by. It's a popular meeting spot, and reservations aren't accepted for parties of fewer than nine, so relax and soak up the wonderful Pine Barrens atmosphere. It's at 2780 Seventh Avenue in Sweetwater, 08037, (609) 965–3285, and open daily 11:30 A.M. to 10:00 P.M. (the bar is open until 1:00 A.M.).

Southern New Jersey seems to be a place that attracts people of vision determined to launch new enterprises. Batsto had Read and his ironworks; Egg Harbor City had Renault and his winery; and just outside Vineland there were whole communities founded by industrious Russian-Jewish immigrants who developed farms and a clothing factory. In Millville a pharmacist named R. T. C. Wheaton set up a glassmaking business that thrives to this day, but Wheaton, Incorporated, now the world's largest family-owned producer of glassware, is not Wheaton's only legacy. His contributions are remembered as well at **Wheaton Village,** a museum and crafts complex that is one of this area's most popular attractions.

The heart of Wheaton Village is the Museum of American Glass, a modern exhibit building that houses a collection of more than 7,500 examples of artistic and utilitarian glassware, ranging from goblets to paperweights, from Mason jars to the world's largest

Carranza Monument

*D*eep in the Pine Barrens, on an unnamed road in desolate Tabernacle Township, a monument adorned with an Aztec eagle and a Spanish inscription marks the spot where a twenty-three-year-old Mexican aviator named Emilio Carranza died on July 13, 1928. Carranza, a Mexican military hero who had made a goodwill flight from Mexico City to Washington and New York, had just left Long Island's Roosevelt Field on what he hoped would be a nonstop return flight when his Ryan Monoplane went down in a thunderstorm. His body was returned to Mexico—and his final, fatal flight was commemorated with what surely must be New Jersey's least-visited monument.

bottle. The museum traces the development of trends in American household glassware, from the roughly crafted glass of colonial times, through the gorgeous stained-glass creations of Louis Comfort Tiffany, to today's handcrafted and mass-produced articles.

In the re-created 1888 Wheaton Glass Factory, artisans employ traditional skills to fashion vases, pitchers, bottles, and other useful and ornamental articles, all of which are for sale in the Wheaton Village stores. For an extra charge one of Wheaton's craftspersons will even guide you as you shape molten glass into your own paperweight.

Other Wheaton Village attractions include the Down Jersey Folklife Center, focusing on the rich and diverse traditions of New Jersey's eight southern counties; an old-time general store, stocked with museum-quality wares that aren't for sale and penny candy that is; a

Craftsmen demonstrate the art of glassblowing at
the Wheaton Glass Factory.

Take a Hike

The well-marked 50-mile Batona Trail wanders through the heart of the Pine Barrens, passing near Batsto Village and connecting Wharton State Forest, Lebanon State Forest, and Bass River State Forest. For a camping permit (issued only for designated sites), contact one of the State Forest offices.

nineteenth-century Tin Shop, with a working resident tinsmith; the Stained Glass Studio, with artists-in-residence using traditional techniques; an 1876 schoolhouse; demonstrations of pottery making, glass lampworking, and wood carving; and The Gallery of American Craft, which features one-of-a-kind American crafts, with a series of special exhibitions that change regularly throughout the year. The 1897 Palermo Railroad Station, typical of rural depots of its era, is more than just a static exhibit—it's a station where you can board a train pulled by the *C. P. Huntington,* a half-scale replica of an 1863 Southern Pacific wood burner. The ³/₄-mile trip circles the museum grounds.

Wheaton Village, 1501 Glasstown Road, Millville 08332, (609) 825–6800, is open daily April through December (except Easter, Thanksgiving, Christmas, and New Year's Day) 10:00 A.M.–5;00 P.M., open Wednesday through Sunday in January, February, and March. Admission is $6.50 for adults, $5.50 for senior citizens, $3.50 for students. Admission fees are reduced January through March.

Are you in the market for a bushel of brussels sprouts? A

peck of potatoes? Head over to the **Vineland Produce Auction**, one of the biggest produce auctions in the East. Everything is locally grown and auctioned off to brokers in large lots. The auction is open to all—even non-bidders—and lasts from one to five hours, depending on the growing season. The auction, on Route 555, 1088 North Main Road, Vineland 08360, (609) 691–0720, is open year-round, every Monday through Thursday, beginning at 11:00 A.M., and Saturday, beginning at 10:30 A.M.

If you're a Matchbox car collector, you know how rare a #41 Ford GT Superfast is. And #22 Pontiac Superfast red. They're on exhibit—along with more than 16,000

Green Tomato Pie

*H*ere's an unusual recipe, using unripe Jersey tomatoes, that was popular long ago down in the Pine Barrens.

Prepare crust for a two-crust pie, using your favorite recipe. Line a pie pan with the bottom crust, and roll out the top crust and have it ready.

Dice six or eight green tomatoes, depending on size (there should be enough to fill the pie shell amply). Cut a half lemon into ⅛-inch pieces, rind and all. Put half of the diced tomatoes into the pie shell, dust with flour, add half of the lemon, and sprinkle with five heaping tablespoons of sugar. Repeat the procedure, finishing with six heaping tablespoons of sugar. Put the top crust on the pie, sealing well. Bake at 400° F. for 30 to 40 minutes, or until the crust is golden. If a toothpick inserted into the pie shows the tomatoes are still firm, cover the rim of the pie with foil to prevent burning as baking completes.

other Matchbox vehicles and products—at the *Matchbox Road Museum & Collector Shoppe* on Pearl Street in Newfield, (609) 697–2800. The museum and shop are usually open daily 9:00 A.M. to 5:00 P.M., but call ahead to make sure they're open. Admission is free.

Delaware Bay Shore

One of the state's finest salt marshes is nestled amidst 5,000 acres of forest and reed thickets at *Dennis Creek Wildlife Management Area* in Dennisville. The mile-long Jake's Landing Road, which leads to the area, passes through a densely pined portion of Belleplain State Forest. The tidal creek, which flows into nearby Delaware Bay, is a popular gathering spot for waterfowl such as Canada geese, goldeneyes, and hooded mergansers and is also an excellent spot for crabbing and fishing.

Cape May National Wildlife Refuge is a welcome resting place for migratory birds about to cross the 12-mile-wide mouth of Delaware Bay. The refuge, now more than 8,000-acres, will ultimately protect 16,700 acres of wildlife habitat on Cape May Peninsula. It's strategically located on the Atlantic Flyway, and its 5-mile stretch along the Bay is recognized as one of the major shorebirding staging areas in North America, providing a critical habitat for hundreds of thousands of migratory birds each year, as well as for other wildlife including forty-two mammal species, fifty-five reptile and amphibian species, and numerous fish and shellfish.

In addition to May and early June, when the shorebirds

arrive (see sidebar, page 219), one of the most exciting times to visit the refuge is during the annual raptor migration in fall, when great numbers of fifteen raptor species, including peregrine falcons, ospreys, and sharp-shinned hawks, land to rest and refuel.

The refuge has two separate divisions: the Delaware Bay Division in Middle Township, which extends along the Delaware Bay; and the Great Cedar Swamp Division, which straddles Dennis and Upper Townships. Stop at Refuge Headquarters to pick up a map and find out the best places for wildlife viewing.

Cape May National Wildlife Refuge Headquarters, 24 Kimbles Beach Road, Cape May Court House 08210, (609) 463–0994, is open weekdays from 8:00 A.M. to 4:00 P.M. If the headquarters is closed when you arrive, pick up a brochure at the information kiosk. The refuge is open daily from sunrise to sunset. Admission is free.

Heading northwest toward the narrow upper part of Delaware Bay, it's easy to follow the main roads through Bridgeton and miss one of southern New Jersey's best-kept secrets. This is the village of **Greenwich,** nestled a few miles from the mouth of the Cohansey River and looking for all the world as if it has just been transported from coastal New England. Appearances aside, it does differ in one important respect—it was laid out in the 1680s by John Fenwick, a Quaker. The fine, straight street Fenwick had surveyed was called Ye Greate Street, and so it is called today. This is where the best of Greenwich's early buildings are. These include the 1730 brick **Nicholas Gibbon House,** with an interior hardly altered over 250 years; the 1771 **Friends'**

Meeting House; and the *Sheppard House,* facing the Cohansey River at the foot of Ye Greate Street. The oldest part of this last structure dates from 1683. From this point a ferry was operated across the Cohansey River from 1767 to 1838. On nearby Market Lane there's a monument to a 1774 event that is as suggestive of New England as the local architecture; here a gang of firebrands, disguised to look like Indians (just as their Boston Tea Party counterparts were), burned a consignment of English tea.

Tours of the colonial homes and other historic buildings of Greenwich are given at various times throughout the year; the Gibbon House is open on a somewhat more regular basis. For information contact the Cumberland County Historical Society (headquartered in the Gibbon House), P.O. Box 16, Ye Greate Street, Greenwich 08323, (609) 451–8454 or (609) 455–4055.

In 1638 a company of Swedes and Finns landed in the New World and set up a structure called Fort Elfsborg, near present-day Salem. The fort didn't last long, but the Scandinavian influence has survived in southern New Jersey to this day. In 1988, to commemorate the 350th anniversary of the first Swedish settlement in America, the New Sweden Company, Inc. erected *New Sweden Farmstead/Museum* in nearby Bridgeton. The farmstead is an exact reproduction of a seventeenth-century farmstead built by the early Swedish and Finnish colonists. It consists of seven log structures: a blacksmith shop, a storehouse, a threshing barn, a stable, a residence, a barn, and a sauna/smokehouse. Construction was supervised by a technical assistance team from Sweden, and most of the furnishings are authentic.

Red Knots

*T*here aren't too many places to put up for the night along New Jersey's Delaware Bay shore, and aside from a few steamed crab stands, there aren't many places to pull off the road for lunch, either. But each May, hungry travelers by the tens of thousands descend upon the Delaware beaches for a much-needed rest and a big, nourishing meal. These are the migratory shorebirds called red knots, and they are heading north from their South American wintering grounds to Canada's subarctic tundra, where they nest and breed. The birds' New Jersey banquet consists of a superabundance of horseshoe crab eggs, freshly laid in the wet sand. It's been estimated that if it weren't for the migrating shorebirds and their need for a midflight protein binge, New Jersey would be paved with horseshoe crabs. And if anything happened to the bay's ecological balance to decimate the population of those primitive creatures, the red knots and other shorebird species would be seriously imperiled.

New Sweden Farmstead/Museum is at City Park on Mayor Aiken Drive off Commerce Street. For more information contact The New Sweden Farmstead/ Museum, Inc., 50 East Broad Street, Bridgeton 08302, (800) 319–3379 (recorded information). The farmstead is open from mid-May through early September. Call for hours and admission costs.

Also at City Park is the *Cohanzick Zoo,* New Jersey's first public zoo and one of the few in the United States that operates without an admission charge. Free admission, however, hasn't affected the quality or quantity of the exhibits; all the animals you'd expect to see are here. For information call (609) 455–3230, extension 242 or 262. The zoo is open daily 8:00 A.M.–5:00 P.M.

The Bridgeton Hall of Fame All Sports Museum, dedicated to individuals and teams of all sports from southern New Jersey, exhibits a huge collection of photos, equipment, scrapbooks, and trophies. A Golden Glove belonging to baseball Hall of Famer Willie Mays is on display here, as are trophies of Olympic athlete John Borican. Baseball stars "Goose" Goslin and Sparky Lyle and boxing legend Rocky Graziano are remembered. It's on Burt Avenue and Babe Ruth Drive, Bridgeton 08302, (609) 451–7300. Open in fall and winter Monday through Friday, 10:00 A.M.–noon and 1:00–3:00 P.M., and in spring and summer, Tuesday through Saturday, 10:00 A.M.–2:00 P.M. Admission is free.

In the spring of 1944 Charles Franklin Seabrook, founder of the largest processor of frozen food in the world, invited a Japanese Relocation Committee to visit South Jersey. He needed workers, and the more than 110,000 Japanese Americans interned in camps because they were deemed "enemy aliens" were eligible for farm work as a result of the War Relocation Authority's seasonal leave policy. Seabrook offered the Japanese jobs, and during the next two years more than 2,500 came from ten relocation centers nationwide.

The farm, which operated around the clock and packed one hundred million pounds of frozen, canned, and dehydrated vegetables a year, also supplemented its workforce with workers from other countries, including Estonia, Romania, Germany, Scotland, Puerto Rico, and the Caribbean. In the 1940s and 1950s it was the most culturally diverse rural area in the country. In 1994, on the fiftieth anniversary of the arrival of the Japanese Americans, the *Seabrook Educational and Cultural*

Center was opened to preserve Seabrook's rich history.

Exhibits at the center focus on three major areas: the historical role that the Seabrook Farms Company played in the area's settlement and employment; the various ethnic groups who settled and/or worked there; and community activity. Among the displays at the center are a large-scale model of what the village looked like in the 1950s, photographs, and oral histories.

The Seabrook Educational and Cultural Center, Upper Deerfield Township Municipal Building, Highway 77, Seabrook 08302, (609) 451–8393, is open Monday through Thursday (except on holidays) 9:00 A.M. to 2:00 P.M.

The *A. J. Meerwald,* a Delaware Bay oyster schooner built in Dorchester, New Jersey in 1928, sets sail from various ports along the Delaware River from May

Sounds of Silence

*W*e drove 5-miles east from Batsto, the restored iron-forge community in the heart of the Pine Barrens, along a dead-straight sand track that was a masterpiece of eighteenth-century surveying. Stopping at a place the map called Washington, we found nothing more than a sand-paved intersection, with a stand of pines at its center, from which other roads went nowhere through the trees. Stagecoaches once stopped here. There were taverns and schools. We got out of the car and looked into the forest, and stood still long enough to surprise a white-tailed deer. The wind gusted; there was a dry whisper of pine needles. We had found the eye of the Jersey storm, here in abandoned Washington, and save for that whisper it was a place of unearthly and un-Jerseylike quiet.

through September. The public sailings are a part of the Delaware Bay Schooner Project, whose mission is to help educate the public about the culture, history, and natural resources of the Delaware Estuary. The ports she sails in and out of include Bivalve, Philadelphia, Ocean City, and Cape May (and, in September, Wilmington). Both daytime and sunset sails are offered, and fares range from $18 to $35. The project is headquartered in Bivalve, which is also home to its **Delaware Bay Museum.** For a schedule and/or information, contact: Delaware Bay Schooner Project, 2800 High Street, Port Norris (Bivalve) 08349, (609) 785–2060.

In 1836 Josiah Reeve, an engineer and shipbuilder, built a Greek Revival home of red brick in the tiny village of Alloway. Today the lovingly restored **Josiah Reeve House,** with its unusual, freestanding spiral staircase and authentically furnished guest rooms, is a great place to stay while you're exploring Salem County, which has more pre–Revolutionary War homes than any other county in the state. The B&B is at North Greenwich Street (P.O. Box 501), Alloway 08001, (609) 935–5640.

Contrary to the sign in his shop, Bob Dorrell doesn't really sell muskrat meat at **Old Alloway Merchandise.** The Sloan's Liniment, Quinine Tar, and Cudahy's lamb livers on the shelves aren't for sale, nor is the tin of saltines, baked before World War II. And there's no charge for the main product Bob is peddling—nostalgia. This circa 1830s general store is crammed with merchandise shoppers expected to see on the shelves over the years. Happily for shoppers, Bob does have a 1927 National cash register to ring up items that are for sale: things like reproduction antiques, penny candy, porcelain and Lee Middleton and Bradley dolls,

Preserved Lands

*I*n December 1997 the New Jersey chapter of the Nature
Conservancy announced that it had established its first
preserve in Ocean County: a 3,500-acre pineland site that is
home to unique dwarf pines as well as the endangered Pine
Barren gentian and northern pine snake. Forked River
Mountain Preserve, made possible by a private donation from
the Leone family, is the chapter's twenty-second New Jersey
nature sanctuary. For information about the site or the
Conservancy, write them at 200 Pottersville Road, Chester
07930; (908) 879–7262.

and gourmet jam. The store, on the corner of Main and
Greenwich Streets, Alloway 08001, (800) 230–4560, is
open Monday, Tuesday, Thursday, and Saturday 10:00
A.M.–5:30 P.M.; Wednesday, 10:00 A.M.–3:00 P.M.; and
Friday 10:00 A.M.–7:00 P.M.; closed Sunday.

Following what is now no longer the bay but the
Delaware River proper, we come to **Salem,** at one time
the site of Fort Elfsborg and later, like Greenwich, settled
by Quakers (1675) associated with the colonial
enterprise of John Fenwick and William Penn. Feisty
little Peter Stuyvesant, the Dutch master of New
Amsterdam (later New York) and the new Netherland
colony, rousted the Swedes from their New Jersey
holdings in 1655; little did he know that he was merely
the middle fish in a gulp-gulp-gulp scenario. The big
fish, of course, was dear Britannia.

Many years later Salem City was the site of an event
important to the future development of New Jersey. One
day in 1820 a man named Robert Gibbon Johnson—a

descendant of the Gibbons who built the fine brick house on Ye Greate Street in Greenwich—walked up the steps of **Salem Court House,** turned to face a gathered crowd, and ate a tomato. He *ate a tomato,* fresh from his own garden, right before a horror-stricken multitude that fully expected him to crumple dead on the spot. Johnson proved his point: tomatoes weren't poisonous. The way was clear for New Jersey—with a little help from as-yet-unarrived Neapolitans, who already knew how good *pomodori* were—to take its rightful place as tomato grower of the world, pizza maker, stacker of cans ... *pace,* Carl Sandburg.

You can still see the courthouse where this landmark event took place. Much altered and added to over the years, it still stands at the corner of Broadway and Market Street, downtown. If you care to go inside, it's open from 9:00 A.M.–noon and 1:00–4:00 P.M. on weekdays. There is no tomato monument, but since the building represents an amalgam of styles from 1817 to 1908, it does offer more than passing interest in its own right. There is, however, a tomato festival in Salem. Held in late September, it's appropriately named after Robert Gibbon Johnson. For information call the Salem Chamber of Commerce at (609) 935–1415.

If there is a spiritual center to Salem, and a place best suited for beginning a walking tour to take in some of its more than sixty colonial and Victorian-era homes, the **Friends Burying Ground,** on West Broadway opposite Oak Street (with its many fine Victorian homes), is surely the place. Here, where many of the earliest settlers of Salem and the lower Delaware Valley lie buried, stands the majestic **Salem Oak.** Estimated to

The Salem Oak, a subject of legends, stands as the sole survivor of a great forest that once covered the Salem town site.

be at least 600 years old, this white oak is the last of the vast forest of trees that covered the site of Salem town when John Fenwick arrived. According to legend this is the tree beneath which Fenwick sat when he signed his initial treaty with the leaders of the local Delaware Indian tribe. When last measured, the Salem Oak stood 88 feet tall, a dimension easily matched by the spread of its branches. The trunk is 30 feet in circumference.

The best source of information on the historic houses of Salem, including maps and pamphlets for a self-guided walking tour, is the Salem County Historical Society. Every other spring the society sponsors an open house, taking in most of the town's important sites. For information contact the society at 79–83 Market Street, Salem 08079, (609) 935–5004.

At *Finn's Point National Cemetery* there are markers

in memory of 2,704 men who died during the Civil War; 2,436 of them were Confederate soldiers who had been interred at a prison camp on nearby Pea Patch Island. Many of them had been captured at the Battle of Gettysburg. There are two monuments here: In 1879, the U.S. government erected a marble memorial to the memory of Union soldiers interred here who died while serving as guards at the camp; and in 1936, a Grecian-type, columned cupola was placed over it. In 1910 the government inscribed the names of the Confederate dead on bronze plates and affixed them to the base of an 85-foot obelisk-type structure of reinforced concrete with Pennsylvania white granite facing.

In the northwest corner of the cemetery, thirteen white marble headstones mark the burial places of World War II German prisoners of war who died while in custody

Lyme Disease

A s New Jersey's deer population increases, so does the number of deer ticks, which can cause Lyme disease. To reduce your chances of being bitten , follow these precautions:

- *wear loose-fitting, light-colored clothing that will help you to see the ticks more easily. A long-sleeved shirt and hat also are recommended;*

- *stay on trails and keep out of densely foliated areas;*

- *leave as little skin exposed as possible.*

If you do find a tick on you, don't panic. Pull it off slowly, making sure to remove it entirely. If you suspect you've been bitten, check with your physician.

at Fort Dix. And in another section are markers for fifty veterans who served in World War II, Korea, or Vietnam.

The cemetery was at one point a small part of the Finn's Point Military Reservation, erected by the government in 1896 in anticipation of the Spanish-American War. The name was changed to Fort Mott in 1897 in honor of Major General Gershom Mott, commander of the New Jersey Volunteers during the Civil War. Today, visitors can tour the fortification at Fort Mott State Park, as well as the cemetery. For information contact Fort Mott State Park, Box 543, R.D. 3, Salem 08079, (609) 935–3218.

Should you decide to spend the night in Salem, stop in at the red brick, three-story 1856 *Richard Woodnutt House Bed and Breakfast.* The rooms are moderately priced and you might get to sleep in a bed hand-carved in 1854. The B&B is at 29 Market Street, (609) 935–4175.

Southern New Jersey might seem an incongruous place to find a professional rodeo, but every Saturday night between Memorial Day and late September, *Cowtown Rodeo* in Woodstown hosts some of the finest riding east of the Mississippi by both cowboys and cowgirls. The rodeo is on Route 40 (mailing address: Route 2, Box 23A), Woodstown 08098, (609) 769–3200. Gates open at 6:00 P.M., and the show starts at 7:30 P.M.; tickets are $10.00 for adults and $6.00 for children under twelve years of age.

The continental menu changes with the seasons at *Old Swedes Inn* in Swedesboro, but almost everything else in the inn has been restored and historically preserved to resemble, as closely as possible, the original 1771 structure. Some of the appointments are a bit more modern: The hammered tin ceiling in the dining room and the mahogany mirror in the porch room are only one hundred years old. The inn, at 301 Kings Highway, (609) 467–2052, serves lunch Wednesday to Friday 11:30 A.M.–2:30 P.M.; dinner nightly 5:30–10:00 P.M.; Sunday brunch noon–2:30 P.M.; and Sunday dinner noon–9:00 P.M.

The tiny village of *Mullica Hill* is a mecca for lovers of antiques and crafts. Residents have turned their homes, or at least part of them, into shops, and now more than seventy line Main Street (Route 45), selling everything from samplers to homemade quilts to Depression glass. The *Dolls, Toys, and Free Museum,* at 34 South Main Street, buys, sells, and repairs dolls, toys, and carousel horses. The museum is open Friday through Sunday, noon–5:00 P.M. and "weekdays by chance." At *Murphy's Loft,* 53 North Main Street, you can browse through 40,000 used, out-of-print, and collectible books. The bookshop is open Wednesday through Sunday 10:00 A.M.–6:00 P.M. *Paper Americana,* One South Main Street, sells eighteenth-century and Civil War newspapers; it's open daily 11:00 A.M.–5:00 P.M. The *Old Arizona Shop,* at 19 South Main Street, sells objects from the Southwest, including pottery, kachina dolls, and Indian blankets; open Wednesday through Sunday. The *Harrison House* serves breakfast, lunch, dinner, late-night snacks, and home-baked goods daily 6:00 A.M.–midnight. For a map or more information, contact Mullica Hill Merchants Association, P.O. Box 235, Mullica Hill 08062, (609) 881–6800.

In the mood to do some picking? Gloucester County is loaded with U-Pick-It Farms. To mention just a few: *Mood's Farm Market,* Route 77, Mullica Hill, (609)

478–2500, for apples, blackberries, blueberries, cherries, grapes, nectarines, pears, plums, raspberries, and snap beans; closed Sundays. *U-Pick,* at the junction of Route 45 and Route 538, Mullica Hill, (609) 478–2864 for peaches, apples, snap beans, okra, black-eyed peas, and eggplants; open daily in season. *Patane's Farm,* 100 Democrat Road, Gibbstown, (609) 423–2726, for cantaloupes, cucumbers, eggplants, squash, tomatoes, turnip greens, peppers, and watermelons. Call ahead to see what's in season.

The oldest log cabin in the United States, believed to have been built shortly after the first Swedish settlers arrived in this country, is the *C. A. Nothnagle Log House* in Gibbstown. Although the actual year of construction is unknown, it is estimated to have been built between 1638 and 1643. The cabin, attached to the home of Doris and Harry Rink, is at 406 Swedesboro Road. The Rinks are generally available to show folks around, but do call ahead, (609) 423–0916, to make sure they're home.

Snake Snackin'

Rattlesnakes were a major threat to early settlers. To protect themselves when they knew they'd be passing through snake country, they'd sometimes drive several hogs in front of them. The hungry swine, protected by coats of bristles and a lining of fat, would scarf up the snakes like popcorn. In the absence of a hog, it is recommended that those who confront an angry rattler back away.

Camden Region

Like it or not, many of South Jersey's Quakers were dragged into the upheaval of the American Revolution. James Whitall and his wife, Ann, kept a comfortable farm along the Jersey side of the Delaware, just 5 miles south of Philadelphia. Their house and land along the river bluffs may have seemed ideally situated in peacetime, but for many of the same reasons, it became a strategic site once hostilities began. The Continentals, wishing to defend the heights of Red Bank (not to be confused with the city of Red Bank, near the Atlantic coast), appropriated James Whitall's apple orchard for the construction of Fort Mercer, and commandeered part of the house itself for the officer's quarters. The immediate British threat was not only from the occupied city of Philadelphia, but from the warships that patrolled the Delaware. The rebels were especially concerned that the naval and land forces not be allowed to unite.

On October 22, 1777, as Rhode Island volunteers were still finishing the earthwork defenses of *Fort Mercer*, 1,200 British and Hessian troops attacked the rear of the fort. Inside were only 400 Americans, but they had been warned of the attack by Jones Cattell, who ran from Haddonfield to alert the Continental commander, Colonel Christopher Greene. Colonel Greene ordered his troops—many of them free blacks—to wait until the last possible minute to fire. Just as the Hessians reached the base of the earthen ramparts, Greene's men let fly a ferocious volley of grapeshot and musket balls. Four hundred Hessians fell dead or wounded. Again they tried; again they were repulsed. As he lay dying, the

Hessian commander, Count Donop, supposedly told his American captors, "I die a victim of my ambition and the avarice of my sovereign."

The pair of unsuccessful Hessian charges upon Fort Mercer lasted barely a half hour, but the engagement between barge mounted American guns and the British warships in the river carried on into the next day. Ann Whitall had tried to ignore the violence flaring all around her, and she continued her spinning in a room on the second floor of her home. When a British cannonball pierced the upper north area of the attic wall and rolled downstairs to where she was sitting, it is said Ann scolded the British, saying: "If thee would not fight; thee would not hurt." Later when her house was requisitioned to serve as a field hospital, she worked hard to nurse all of the wounded.

Despite the success of Fort Mercer's defenders, General Washington eventually decided that he could not afford to commit enough men to the task of maintaining it. After the position was abandoned, the British overran and looted Whitall's property. The Quaker billed the Continental Congress for compensation, which was never received.

From the return of James and Ann in 1778 until 1897, three generations of Whitalls lived in the stout stone-and-brick house on the heights above the Delaware. The surrounding property was acquired by the United States government in 1872 (hence the name of the municipality—National Park, New Jersey), but it was turned over to Gloucester County authorities in 1905. Since then it has been managed as a park in commemoration of the Battle of Red Bank.

Aside from the preserved and partially reconstructed earthworks of Fort Mercer, the principal attraction of **Red Bank Battlefield** is the recently restored **Whitall House**. Today the house looks much as it did in the peaceful days before the Revolution, when James Whitall ran his farm from the little first-floor office that faced the river; elsewhere within the 1748 structure (the stone portion is said to have been built by Swedish settlers even earlier) are a formal parlor, a "great" room, with a large hearth; a huge kitchen located in the stone wing; and bedrooms. The furnishings are all in keeping with the period, as are the kitchen gardens and small orchard outside. On a late October day, the windfallen apples give off their winey smell, a welcome change from the stench of black powder and blood.

The Red Bank Battlefield, 100 Hessian Avenue, National Park 08063, (609) 853–5120, is open all year during daylight hours. The Whitall House is open April through September, Wednesday through Friday, 9:00 A.M.–4:00 P.M., and weekends, 1:00–4:00 P.M. Donations are accepted.

In Camden stands the **Walt Whitman House,** where the Good Grey Poet lived from 1884 until his death in 1892. This two-story frame building is the only home Walt Whitman ever owned, and he was able to pay the $1,750 that it cost only because of the unexpectedly large amount of money he earned from sales of the seventh edition of *Leaves of Grass.* Whitman had been boarding with his brother in Camden; when he moved into his own house, he had no furnishings other than a bed, a chair, and his books. Partially paralyzed from a series of strokes, he needed a housekeeper as well as a household.

He found both when he engaged a widow, Mrs. Mary Davis, to move in with her own furniture and see to the cooking and cleaning in return for free rent. Whitman himself was by then a poor man, living largely on the generosity of his friends for the last eight years of his life.

Visitors to the Whitman House can see the poet's sparse furnishings, many of his books, and an interesting array of memorabilia, including photographs, letters, and documents.

The Walt Whitman House, 330 Mickle Boulevard, Camden 08103, (609) 964–5383, is open Wednesday through Saturday 10:00 A.M.–noon and 1:00–5:00 P.M., and Sunday 1:00–4:00 P.M. Admission is free.

If you want to make a pilgrimage to Whitman's grave, head over to **Harleigh Cemetery,** which donated a plot to the poet. He paid for the mausoleum, which he shares with his mother and brother. There's a black granite monument with his likeness on it, and his own elegy:

> *I bequeath myself to the dirt to grow from the grass I love,*

> *If you want me again look for me under your boot soles.*

Haiku poet Nick Virgilio is also buried here in a grave

Pass the Popcorn

In 1933 the world's first drive-in movie theater opened its "doors" in Camden, featuring Wife Beware *with Adolphe Menjou.*

overlooking the lake. A lectern is etched with his poem "Lily/out of the water/out of itself."

The Harleigh Cemetery, 1640 Haddon Avenue, Camden 08103, (609) 963–0122, is open daily from 7:30 A.M.–4:30 P.M.

Another Camden site worth a visit is **Pomona Hall,** headquarters and museum of the Camden County Historical Society. Pomona Hall is a handsome Georgian brick structure, built in 1726 by prominent Quaker Joseph Cooper, Jr., and expanded in 1788 by his descendant Marmaduke Cooper. Inside are fine examples of eighteenth- and nineteenth-century furnishings and colonial kitchen equipment. The holdings of the society's adjoining museum include Indian artifacts, Civil War memorabilia, representative tools associated with preindustrial crafts, fire-fighting equipment, and antique toys. A special exhibit chronicles the days, just after the turn of the century, when Camden was the home of the Victor Talking Machine Company. If you've ever heard the voice of Enrico Caruso transcend the decades through the medium of a brittle black disk, you can bet that it was recorded at the Victor studios in Camden.

The Camden County Historical Society's Museum and Pomona Hall and Library, Park Boulevard and Euclid Avenue, Camden 08103, (609) 964–3333, is open Tuesday and Thursday 12:30–4:30 P.M., Sunday 1:00–5:00 P.M. Admission is $2.00 for adults, $1.00 for senior citizens, and 75 cents for students seventeen and over; children through age sixteen are admitted free.

The New Jersey State Aquarium in Camden (One

Springtime Posies

*E*ach April in the Pine Barrens the sand myrtle, a rare, small plant with dark, boxlike leaves and white flowers, blossoms for several weeks.

Riverside Drive 08103, 609–365–3300), is hardly off the beaten path. With parking for 2,200 cars, it's one of the state's major tourist attractions. Nevertheless, it's easy to miss an extremely pleasurable side trip that departs from the aquarium—the *Riverbus.* This ferry crosses the Delaware River in ten minutes and deposits passengers at Penn's Landing in Philadelphia. For a schedule and/or information: Riverbus, Inc., P.O. Box 327, Camden 08101, (609) 354–1400 or (800) 634–4027.

Amid the urban bustle of Cherry Hill sits *Barclay Farmstead*—a living-history museum dedicated to preserving a way of life that is quickly disappearing in New Jersey. The centerpiece of the thirty-two-acre farm on the north branch of the Cooper River is a three-story brick Federal farmhouse, built in the 1820s and completely furnished with period antiques. There are also an operating forge, barn, and blacksmith shop; a corn crib; a Victorian springhouse; and a museum shop. The farmstead, at 209 Barclay Lane, Cherry Hill 08034, (609) 795–6225, is open Tuesday through Friday 9:00 A.M.–4:00 P.M.; closed Mondays and national holidays. An admission fee is charged.

Near Barclay Farmstead on Covered Bridge Road is *Scarborough Covered Bridge,* one of two remaining covered bridges in the state, and the first to be built in New Jersey in ninety-three years. It was dedicated on February 14, 1959.

The Shrimp Vindaloo at the **Tandoor Palace** is spicy and hot, just the way a good vindaloo should be. Less-intrepid diners can choose from other Indian dishes, such as Chicken Tikka or Lamb Rogan Josh. Everything is delicious and inexpensive. The restaurant, in Plaza 30 Shopping Center, 328 White Horse Pike, Clementon 08021, (609) 435–1234, is open for lunch daily and for dinner every night except Monday.

It's rumored that the Jersey Devil—a phantom beast that has plagued South Jersey since colonial times—has been spotted in the area of the **Jackson Museum,** housed in a 150-year-old schoolhouse. The schoolhouse was formerly on the property of Six Flags Great Adventure. In 1984 Six Flags donated the building to the Jackson Heritage Preservation Society, who paid to have it moved to a site behind the town's municipal building. Today the museum exhibits artifacts from the inland, forested section of Ocean County. The museum, open by appointment, is on Don Connor Boulevard, Jackson 08527, (732) 928–1200, extension 200.

For thousands of years people of the Powhatan nation have inhabited the coastal areas of the mid-Atlantic. The oldest written treaty in North America (1646) was between the Powhatan Confederacy and England. The **American Indian Heritage Museum,** on the Rankokus Reservation, re-creates the history of these people and the part they played in shaping the United States. The museum tour includes a visit to the outdoor re-creation of a traditional ancestral woodland village and an opportunity to see live buffalo. The art gallery exhibits contemporary paintings, sculpture, pottery, drawings, photographs, and wood carvings. The museum, on the Rankokus Reservation, Rancocas Road, Rancocas (mailing address: P.O. Box 225, Rancocas 08073), (609) 261–4747, is open Saturday and by appointment on Tuesday and Thursday, 10:00 A.M.–3:00 P.M. Admission is $4.00 for adults, $3.00 for senior citizens, and $2.00 for children.

PLACES TO STAY
IN SOUTHERN NEW JERSEY

HILTON CHERRY HILL
2369 West Marlton Pike, Route 70, Cherry Hill 08002; (800) 445–8667 or (609) 665–6666; fax (609) 662–1414

ISAAC HILLIARD HOUSE B & B
31 Hanover Street, Pemberton 08068; (800) 371–0756 or (609) 894–0756

THE QUEEN ANNE B & B INN
44 West End Avenue, Haddonville 08033; (609) 428–2195; fax (609) 354–1273

RAMADA INN AND CONFERENCE CENTER
399 Monmouth Street, Hightstown 08520; (609) 448–7000

THE VICTORIAN LADY
301 West Main Street, Moorestown 08057; (609) 235–4988

WEST DEPTFORD INN
Exit 20, Route 295, West Deptford 08086; (800) 528–1234 or (609) 848–4111; fax (609) 845–8977

PLACES TO EAT
IN SOUTHERN NEW JERSEY

AL KHIMAH
1426 East Marlton Pike, Cherry Hill; (609) 427–0888
(Moroccan and Middle Eastern cuisine)

BARNSBORO INN
699 Main Street, Barnsboro; (609) 468–3557

BRADDOCK'S TAVERN
39 South Main Street, Medford;
(609) 654–1604

THE INN AT SUGAR HILL
5704 Mays Landing–Somers
Point Road, Mays Landing;
(609) 625–2226

LA CAMPAGNE
312 Kresson Road, Cherry Hill;
(609) 429–7647

LA FAMILIA SONSINI
202 Old Marlton Pike, Medford;
(609) 654–5217

OLGA'S DINER
Routes 70 and 73, Marlton;
(609) 596–1700

PACIFIC GRILL
Village II Shopping Center, 1200
South Church Street and
Academy Drive, Mount Laurel;
(609) 778–0909

TULIPANO NERO
3747 Church Road, Mount
Laurel; (609) 235–6955

OTHER ATTRACTIONS
IN SOUTHERN NEW JERSEY

AMALTHEA CELLARS
267A Hayes Mill Road, Atco
08004; (609) 768–8585

FINNS POINT LIGHTHOUSE
Supawna Meadows National
Wildlife Refuge, Fort Mott and
Lighthouse Roads,
Pennsville 08079; (609)
935–1487

INDIAN KING TAVERN MUSEUM
233 Kings Highway East,
Haddonfield 08033; (609)
429–6792

NAIL HOUSE MUSEUM
1 Mayor Aitken Drive, Bridgeton
City Park, Bridgeton 08302;
(609) 455–4100

**OLD SWEDES TRINITY
EPISCOPAL CHURCH**
Kings Highway and Church
Street, Swedesboro 08085; (609)
467–1227

POTTER'S TAVERN
West Broad Street, Bridgeton
08302; (609) 451–4802

RENAULT GLASS MUSEUM
72 North Bremen Avenue, Egg
Harbor City 08215; (609)
965–2111

**TOWNE OF HISTORIC SMITHVILLE
AND THE VILLAGE GREEN**
Route 9 and Moss Mill Road,
Smithville 08201; (609)
652–4040

Selected Regional Information Centers, Chambers of Commerce, and Visitor Centers in Southern New Jersey

Delaware River Region Tourism Council,
1821 Old Cuthbert Road, Cherry Hill 08034,
(609) 429–6111

Pinelands Commission,
P.O. Box 7, New Lisbon 98064,
(609) 894–9342

Salem County Department of Economic Development,
(609) 935–7510, ext. 532

Index

About the Authors

William G. Scheller was born in Paterson, New Jersey, where several generations of his family worked in the local locomotive, silk, and aircraft industries. He attended Paterson schools and both St. Peter's Preparatory School and St. Peter's College in Jersey City.

Mr. Scheller is the author of sixteen books, including *New York: Off the Beaten Path, Country Walks Near New York*, and *The Hudson River Valley*. His articles have appeared in the *Washington Post Magazine,* the *Christian Science Monitor, Islands,* and *National Geographic Traveler.* Along with his friend and occasional collaborator, New York photographer Chris Maynard, Mr. Scheller was profiled in a *New Yorker* "Talk of the Town" piece for having canoed the length of New Jersey's Passaic River and for circumnavigating (also by canoe) Manhattan Island. The two also collaborated on *Manifold Destiny*, a guide to cooking on car engines.

Kay Scheller is a co-author of *New York: Off the Beaten Path* (third edition) and a contributor to National Geographic's *Crossing America,* Fodor's *Boston,* and Fodor's *New England.* Ms. Scheller was a co-author of the *New England* volume in National Geographic Society's *Driving Guides to America* series.

The Schellers live in northern Vermont with their young son.

Discover hidden places all over the United States and Canada with the Off the Beaten Path™ series. Devoted to travelers with a taste for the unique, these guides feature out-of-the-way discoveries that resonate with local color and touch the true heart of the regions they cover. Globe Pequot offers an Off the Beaten Path™ guide for all fifty states!

Interested in more New Jersey adventures? Try these favorites from Globe Pequot:

Guide to the Jersey Shore   *$12.95*
The delights of coastal New Jersey are covered, from the beaches to the boardwalks.

Great Family Vacations: Northeast   *$14.95*
Twenty-four fun-filled vacations for the entire family!

Canoeing the Jersey Pine Barrens   *$11.95*
Detailed river descriptions and history of this coastal plain region of southern New Jersey.

Short Bike Rides in New Jersey   *$12.95*
Delightful short and moderate tours for the casual cyclist.

To order these Globe Pequot books or to request a catalog, call 1-800-243-0495, fax 1-800-820-2329 or write The Globe Pequot Press, P.O. Box 833, Old Saybrook, CT 06475. Visit our website at http://www.globe-pequot.com.